COMPLEX LIFE: NONMODERNITY AND THE EMERGENCE OF COGNITION AND CULTURE

Complex Life: Nonmodernity and the Emergence of Cognition and Culture

ALAN DEAN
The University of Hull

Ashgate

Aldershot • Brookfield USA • Singapore • Sydney

Published by
Ashgate Publishing Ltd
Gower House
Croft Road
Aldershot
Hants GU11 3HR
England

Ashgate Publishing Company
Old Post Road
Brookfield
Vermont 05036
USA

Ashgate website: http://www.ashgate.com

British Library Cataloguing in Publication Data
Dean, Alan, Ph. D.
    Complex life : nonmodernity and the emergence of cognition
    and culture
    1. Cognition and culture 2. Human beings 3. Behavior evolution
    4. Ethnophilosophy
    I. Title
    302.1

Library of Congress Catalog Card Number: 99-75539

ISBN 0 7546 1049 7

Printed in Great Britain by
Antony Rowe Ltd, Chippenham, Wiltshire

Contents

Acknowledgements

First of all my thanks go to Mitzi Wakefield for her everlasting patience, encouragement and support. Thanks also to Mark Johnson for timely advice on material culture and the tangled web of human agency, and to all my colleagues in the Department of Sociology and Social Anthropology at Hull University. I am grateful to Stella Richards for keeping many administrative demands at bay during a busy academic year. Particular thanks also to Larry Harrison, Jo Wild and Adrian James. Finally, I am indebted to Susan Whitlock for providing invaluable feedback and guidance during the early stages of writing this book.

Introduction

This book comprises a series of chapters that span ideas relating to human origins, the nature of mind and human agency. As substantive areas there is nothing new in this as considerable empirical and theoretical research has been devoted to these topics over the years. What is perhaps less usual is the fact that a commentary on each of these should appear in the same text as an integrated analysis. Academic research is structured in the main on a disciplinary basis. Each group of social scientists have their own primary focus. Generally it is very unlikely that a social theorist would comment on, say, the classification of human fossil remains, or a phenomenologist pass judgment on some early feature of Australopithecus morphology. Similarly, biologist are not routinely given to cultural analyses nor social anthropologist to commentaries on the evolution of the brain. Each group makes its own contribution to our improving knowledge of ourselves, both individually and collectively.

This has been the way the sciences that relate to human life have been structured for many years, and it is a foolish person who has in the past sought to pass comment on developments in a field outside their own. Of course this is understandable to a marked degree because the vast body of research that comprises a field of knowledge is such that few, if any, would have the time to become an expert in more than one disciplinary area. The number of academic journals seems to increase year by year, as does the volume of books available on any academic subject. Thus, the limited disciplinary focus of most research is not only understandable, but an almost inevitable outcome of continuous improvements in research output. However, the fact that the disciplinary structure of academic life is understandable does not mean that it may not be a limiting factor in the generation of new ideas. Viewing human nature from just one perspective ineyitably restricts the range of ideas that can be considered. There is no doubt that human life is cultural, but it is also biological. Our mental life may be reducible in some degree to individual psychology, but it is also linguistic and thus collective. What can be said about human life from within the boundaries of any one discipline will comprise only a limited selection of the whole, and consequently differing theoretical positions may become to be based on seemingly irreconcilable differences. For example, within evolutionary anthropology and psychology Darwinian natural selection theory holds centre stage in any analysis. In a similarly focused way, poststructuralist social theory is grounded on a particular position regarding the division of nature and culture within human agency. Poststructuralists hold that discourse is transcendent over nature as an agent within human affairs, a position that has stemmed from the general postmodern social theoretical interest in unveiling the contingent and discontinuous character of social and cultural life.

It is understandable that the social sciences have developed in this way given the different focus of each approach. Asking a Foucaldian to reflect upon Darwin's contribution to the human sciences is unlikely to produce a helpful response given that the starting point of their analysis can be found in reflections on power and discourse. Nevertheless, there is a need to find a paradigm that may provide some theoretical bridge between disciplines if limitations within respective fields are to be addressed. Within this book discussion will reveal some of these limitations, such as Foucault's problem with the nature of the subject, the postmodernist rejection of objective knowledge when confronted with contingency and unpredictability, and the lack of evidence of an engagement with human agency on the part of physical anthropology. The attempt within the book is not to answer all such questions, but rather to show how some new approaches in social theory may help disciplines to develop a dialogue richer in scope than the more usual examples of multi-disciplinary work, characterised as it often is by the lack of an integrated framework and a consequent production of abstracted statements about data.

By a new approach I have in mind the increasing attempts to apply complexity theory to the social sciences. Complexity theory can show how contingency, turbulence, unpredictability and nonlinearity in day-to-day life does not stem from the discursive character of human agency, but is instead a feature of the operation of complex systems. Contingency does not mean the end of objectivity, just the separation of this from predictability. Complexity theory shows that just because something is determined it does not mean that outcomes can be predicted in advance. I also have in mind developments in what is becoming to be known as nonmodern social theory. I think it correct to attribute the first use of this term to the work of Bruno Latour, but others are now seeing the usefulness of this approach and beginning to use it as a critique of both modern and postmodern social theory. Nonmodern social theory is grounded in the idea that nature and culture are inseparable. Modernity never conquered nature, nor was it transcended within the postmodern world. As Latour has argued, the human world is otherwise infused with elements that are hybrids of nature and culture (Latour 1993). Complexity theory sits well with nonmodern social theory because it too is based upon the indivisibility of the constituent parts of a system. Within complexity theory what happens at the surface, macro level is seen to be an emergent outcome of great interconnectivity between constituent elements within the system. And for human agency this means interconnectivity between biology, mind, culture and environment.

It is this stance that offers something new in terms of human evolution. Rather than pursuing an analysis of human origins solely in terms of relationships between morphology and environment, complexity theory draws the researcher towards considering the possibility that it may be impossible to unravel completely the intricate pathway of evolution in detail. Many outcomes may have been unexpected consequences of some other earlier changes. This is not to deny the importance of Darwinian natural selection theory, traits would not have endured if they were not adaptive. Indeed one aim of the book is to attempt a synthesis of complexity theory and Darwinian natural selection theory. An attempt that will seek to bring the concept of an exaptation to the fore.

The journey through the ideas presented in this book is thus somewhat different from that usually found in books on either social theory or human origins. It is expected, therefore, that some will like it more than others, and some may not like it at all. Although complexity theory has now been around within quantitative social science for some time, it is new to theoretical sociology and anthropology, so some misgivings are to be expected. I do not think this book provides a final word on the subjects touched upon, but hopefully it will prove to be a modest source of new ideas. Generally social scientists appear trapped at present in either a belief in the post-Enlightenment interest in a predictive science of human life, or in a postmodernists rejection of the possibility of acquiring objective knowledge. A synthesis of Darwinian natural selection theory and complexity theory could provide a new direction for the social sciences. This further development of nonmodern social theory would stress the inseparability of nature and culture as components of human agency.

The book is structured into seven chapters. In chapter one research findings on the evolution of modern humans over approximately the last two million years is presented. This chapter seeks to introduce a complex perspective on the emergence of humankind. Chapter two is focused on the evolutionary emergence of symbolic reasoning. It is argued that encephalisation may be linked to migratory behaviour and subsequent inbreeding between physically dissimilar early human ancestors. Theories of cognitive evolution are considered in chapter three where the role of tool-making as a primary precursor of symbolic reasoning is considered. Attention is also placed on related findings from evolutionary psychology, neuroscience and social anthropology. In chapter four consideration is given to the emergent conditions of cultural life. It is argued that rather than being the result of an evolutionary disjunction with the past, the conditions from which culture arose are grounded in material concerns relating to reproduction and survival. Chapter five extends the argument presented in the previous chapter and develops it further through a detailed analysis of incest taboos. From this it is argued that cultural practices can be seen to be the emergent outcome of an interweaving of environmental conditions, morphology, cognition, sociality and cultural practices. Following on from this discussion, chapter six shows how the analysis presented so far can provide a basis for a critique of both modern and postmodern social theory. A possible synthesis of Darwinian natural selection theory and complexity theory is made explicit and used to provide a re-working of the developing framework of nonmodern social theory. In the final chapter it is argued that the adoption of a nonmodern perspective on the origins of modern humans can offer new insights into the inter-relationship between biology, psychology and culture. Central to this is the status of human agency as an emergent outcome of a complex nature-culture system.

1 From Primate to Human

How long human beings have been around on this planet has concerned scientist and non-scientist for many years. There is an enduring concern in discovering just where it is we all came from, particularly with respect to uncovering the identity of the last common ancestor between us and other apes. In focusing on this problem the academic community and others have produced outstanding results, and it is now generally accepted that the first clearly distinct ancestor of modern humans appeared about 1.7 million years ago. This ancestor was named *Homo erectus*, being the first species to more resemble modern humans physically than have an ape-like form. Less certain, however, is how and where the most human of characteristics, a large and complex brain which facilitated language and self-conscious awareness, arose. It is known the the gradual enlargement of cranial capacity began with *H. erectus*, but why this occurred and how it gave rise to our unique cognitive abilities is not yet completely understood. For some it may have stemmed from tool making, whilst for others the focus is on language and the requirements of social life, but as yet our understanding of this most important outcome of human evolution is incomplete.

It is the purpose of this chapter to introduce the reader to some key ideas and findings on this issue, and on human evolution in general. It is not the intention to provide a comprehensive overview, there are many existing text books which achieve that aim with great skill and scholarship, rather the intention here is to illustrate the complex character of human evolution. That is, to demonstrate that even in the beginning human life followed a path which was intricate and unpredictable. And the best way to begin this intellectual journey is some five or six million years ago, when it is thought that hominids first appeared.

The Emergence of Humankind

As stated above, it is not the objective in this section to provide a detailed review of current thinking on the evolutionary path of the emergence of modern humans. There are many excellent texts available which achieve that task well. Instead the intention here is to provide an overview of some key ideas which will serve to draw attention to the complexity of human evolution and thus the difficulties surrounding any attempts to establish for certain a known chronological or geographic location from which humankind emerged.

There is a long tradition within human origins research to focus attention on morphological characteristics when seeking to unravel the circumstances of the beginnings of our species. The early taxonomists such as Linnaeus in the 18th century and Gray in the 19th century set in place principles for the classification of species which are as authoritative today as they were when first formulated. This work on classification has provided the foundation for a wealth of research on human fossil remains. And this research has led to many analyses that have sought to locate humankind historically in an evolutionary tree. By comparing the presence or absence of certain anatomical features between differing hominid species, various histories of the emergence of modern humans have been put forward. From this research it is generally accepted that the first modern humans emerged in sub-Saharan Africa. Of course in reality the picture is much more complex than that, but before we muddy the waters with a touch of non-linearity a basic overview will be introduced.

Humankind taxonomically is included in the Order Primate within which there are two sub-orders; the Prosimii which includes lemurs, and the Anthropoiddea including, for example, monkeys and apes. Within the Anthropoidea (meaning human like) there are further sub-divisions into Superfamilies, one of which, the Hominiods, includes the great apes and humans. Subsequently, to distinguish humankind from other apes, the Family Hominid was proposed. Thus, presently, the formal classification of humankind is: Order Primates; Suborder Anthropoidea; Superfamily Hominoidea; Family Hominidae. The other great apes are classified within the Family Pongidae.

So, having sketch out this brief classification system it may be appreciated that the task of conceptualising human origins should become easier. What we have to do is trace back the evolutionary path and establish when, both geologically and environmentally in terms of habitat, the Family Hominid diverged from the Family Pongidae.

Some of this work has been carried out over recent years through the analysis of fossil remains, through the use of molecular data and by comparing the genetic material of living hominoids. And from this research it is generally held to be the case that the earliest hominoids diverged about 15 million years ago to form the Asian hominoids and the African hominoids. The orangutan is a living example of an Asian hominoid. Although there is no clear consensus at the present time it is generally held to be the case that the great apes and Hominids diverged around six million years ago, at which time the Hominids became a distinct family. However, some evidence from molecular studies of genetic material suggests that the gorilla diverged much earlier than the chimpanzee, by perhaps several million years (Tobias 1994). Nevertheless, even though that may be the case, it does not change the picture being drawn here, that the direct ancestors of humankind emerged as a distinct species some 6 million or so years ago.

What distinguishes humans from non-humans are a number of generally agreed morphological and behavioural characteristics. The main morphological characteristics are held to be an upright posture and bipedalism, brain enlargement and the development of the cerebral lobes and areas associated with language development, the adaptation of the upper limb from locomotor or climbing usage to increased manipulation of objects, particularly with respect to developments to the hand, the reduction in tooth size, loss of body hair, and changes in skull shape. Also of importance were changes in the upper respiratory tract which provided the basis for the improved vocalisation of hominids compared with other hominoids. In behavioural terms, the important classificatory elements are the use of language, the use of tools and an increased dependence on manufacture and the manipulation of environments for survival. But having classified humans in this way the task is far from complete. The analysis of genetic material or the comparison of hand morphology may allow distinctions to be made between humans and the chimpanzee, but seeking to discover the last common ancestor is a more complex task.

In essence there are two primary tasks to be completed in human origins research. One is to establish the nature of the last common ancestor and complete the evolutionary record from that point to modern humans, and the second is to unfold the quality of the selective pressures from which the depicted adaptations arose. Neither of these tasks has proved easy to achieve in practice. There is great uncertainty as to whether modern humans arose once in Africa, or whether evolutionary events within the hominid Family central to the emergence of modern humans occurred in different geographic locations and at different times. There is also a lack of agreement concerning the characteristics of the habitat from which hominids emerged distinct from other hominoids. At the present time the consensus is that that the dry African savannah is the most likely engendering habitat, though there are others who claim a multi-regional, multi-enivironment model, and there is even a claim that an aquatic environment was the most likely starting point for the development of modern human characteristics (Morgan 1982). Clearly the path of this current analysis is rendered more difficult by such uncertainties. But this very complexity is the key to understanding the broader context of human existence, as will be revealed below. For the present, though, it will be more helpful to the reader if a brief review of the broad strands of human evolution are provided.

The Evolution of the Hominids and the Emergence of *Homo sapien*

The analysis of early human evolution has revealed that it is likely that *Australopithecus afarensis*, which stemmed from early unclassified Australopithcenes, emerged as our most distant known hominid ancestor approximately three to four million years ago. *A. afarensis* (the famous Lucy) had considerable differences in size between males and females. They varied between 1 and 1.7 m in height and 25 to 59 kg in weight. They were bipedal and had a cranial volume between 380 to 450 cc, with an average brain size of 413 cc (Tobias 1994).

Next in the evolutionary line is believed to be *Australopithecus africanus* which appeared about two to three million years ago. *A. africanus* were of different stature than *A. afarensis* at around 1.4 m, and had a larger cranial volume of between 400 to 500 cc. *Africanus* also had smaller incisor teeth and a flatter face than *A. afarensis*. At this point in hominization it is agreed by most that a divergence took place between the Australopithecine genus and an emerging Homo genus. Within the Australopithecus (or *Paranthropus* as some authorities prefer) genus *Australopithecus robustus* emerged around 1 to 2 million years ago, and *Australopithecus boisei* around the same time. *Robustus* had an average height of 1.5 m, weighed an average of 45 kg and had a cranial capacity of 500 to 600 cc housed in a large skull with a distinct skull ridge (a sagittal ridge also found with present day gorillas). *A. boisei* had a very similar morphology, being heavily bodied with a sagittal ridge, a wide jaw and large molars and premolars. Due to the large molar teeth both are thought to have been plant eating species. It is also believed that they may have succeeded the more gracile formed *A. africanus* in response to the effects of glaciation. It is generally held to be the case that a heavier form is more adapted to colder climates than a lighter, taller form.

Homo habilis is the first documented member of the *Homo* genus having appeared sometime between 1.5 and two million years ago. It was with *H. habilis* that signs appeared of a large-scale increase in brain size sign. Compared to *A. africanus* the brain volume had increased by some 40% to an average of approximately 640 cc (Tobias 1994). However, despite this increase in brain size *H. habilis* are not usually considered to be the first humans due to their ape like body proportions, long arms and a short body, relatively small brains when compared to modern humans, comparatively large teeth and a seeming a lack of human behaviour (Stringer and Gamble 1993). However, as Stringer and Gamble (1993) point out, there was more than one type of *H. Habilis*. Fossil remains depict large and small bodied types that may constitute different species. Both types are distinguishable from *A. robustus*, *A. boisei* and the later *Homo erectus*.

H. habilis eventually disappeared around 1.5 million years ago, after the arrival of a new hominid species *Homo erectus*. This hominid had a mean cranial capacity of 930 cc and was taller than earlier appearing hominids, with body proportions similar to that of certain existing African people (Stringer and Gamble 1993; Leakey and Walker 1989) and appeared around 1.7 million years ago). *H. erectus* are thought to be the first hominid species to migrate from Africa. *H. erectus* is known from fossil records to have migrated to Asia, where the skull developed a more robust construction than earlier African types. Asian *H. erectus* had long flattened skulls with a distinct sagittal ridge and an occipital ridge to the rear of the skull (Stringer and Gamble 1993). This migration to Asia occurred approximately one million years ago (Stringer and Gamble 1993), during which time, along with the increased robustness of the skull, cranial capacity increased some 25% to an average of approximately 1100 cc for specimens found in China and Java (Stringer and Gamble 1993; Tobias 1994). The reasons for these changes are not known, though Stringer and Gamble (1993) suggest that the development to a more robust form may have occurred in response to climatic changes in Europe and Asia.

By 700, 000 to 800,000 years ago *H. erectus* was established in the Middle East and southern Europe (Stringer and Gamble 1993), and up to 300,000 years ago could be found widely dispersed in Europe, including Britain and Germany, India, China and Indonesia. As reported by Stringer and Gamble (1993) there is some evidence that in the west *H. erectus* had developed into a species distinct from the more robust Asian *erectus*. It appears from fossil evidence that western *erectus* had cranial volumes matching that of modern humans and less robust skull structures (Rightmire 1990). However many other writers hold that the western type is the result of continuous development in response to climatic differences and that adaptations did not lead to the emergence of a new species.

Perhaps the best known human ancestor is the Neanderthal, which is believed to have evolved in Europe by approximately 230,000 years ago (Stringer and Gamble 1993). Fossil remains, such as those found at Caune de l'Arago in southwest France, suggest that Neanderthals arose from *H. erectus* perhaps some 400,000 years ago. These fossil remains of 60 specimens in total show characteristics of both *H. erectus* and Neanderthals. Other middle Pleistocene fossils found in Swanscombe in the UK and Steinheim in Germany also show characteristics of both Neanderthal and erectus morphology. Taken together the evidence suggests that the evolution of the Neanderthals followed a pattern which resulted in a morphological mosaic in which individuals, perhaps from different geographical regions, had dissimilar combinations of Neanderthal and *erectus* characteristics. Nevertheless, as stated above, by around 230,000 years ago Neanderthals had evolved into a distinct species characterised by a short forearm and lower leg, relatively enlarged front teeth compared with their other teeth (with evidence to suggest that these front teeth were used as a tool to hold objects), long and broad noses when compared to modern humans, a protruding jaw line, and a long and flattened cranium (Trinkaus 1986; Klein 1989; Stringer and Gamble 1993). At some 1300 cc for females and up to about 1700 cc for males, the brain volume of Neanderthals was greater than that of both *H. erectus*, which reached around 1200 cc and modern humans, where the average is between 1200 cc and 1500 cc (Stringer and Gamble 1993). However, although the beginnings of Neanderthals may be largely unproblematic so far as lineage is concerned, their eventual fate is less certain. There are those who claim that Neanderthals were the direct ancestors of modern European humans, whereas others believe that Neanderthals died out around 100,000 to 75,000 years ago as they were replaced by a new wave migration by modern humans.

The emergence of Neanderthals was an exclusively European affair. These species did not emerge in any further east than the Middle East, and even this most easterly presence has not been confirmed. In contrast, in the east a distinct late version of *erectus* appeared in China and Java around 250,000 years ago. This species was eventually transplanted by an archaic modern human which persisted in these areas until about 75,000 years ago when modern humans appeared. The form of this archaic ancestor may perhaps be typified by the fossil remains discovered in 1921 at Broken Hill, Zambia. These 200,000 year old remains reveal a brain volume greater than a typical *erectus*., a robust skull structure but a taller and narrower overall physique. Although the remains appeared to be from more than one specimen, Stringer and Gamble (1993) concluded that although in general the remains are more primitive than either modern humans or Neanderthals, the limb bones suggest a closer relation to the modern form than Neanderthals.

So, at this stage the overall picture of human evolution suggests that from about 1 million to 700,000 years or earlier *H. erectus* migrated from Africa and eventually, by about 500,000 years ago, spread through Asian and Europe. In Europe a relatively gracile *erectus*, mirroring the earliest forms found in Africa in this respect (e.g. West Turkana boy), evolved into a more robust Neanderthal, a process which did not take place in Asia where a more robust form of *erectus* persisted until the emergence of an archaic human from around an estimated 200,000 years ago. Or at least that is the picture described by most current research. However, the data indicate greater complexity than that described so far.

Complexity in the Early Human Evolutionary Process

In principle it is relatively easy for the purposes of illustration to put forward simple hypotheses for early human evolution. It could be argued that the earliest hominids stood up because those that did were more effective in scouting for food or searching for predators. Once on two legs rather than four the possibility for using the fore limbs for other than locomotion became possible. Greater articulation of simple tools in defence, mate-seeking or food gathering imparted a selective advantage, hence such traits became subject to natural selection. Subsequently, the more intelligent of the species, those more effective at manipulating their environment, were more successful at these behaviours and thus experienced better survival and reproduction rates. Hence, over time, brain volume increased by way of selective pressure on appropriate cognitive and behavioural traits.

It is from such reasoning (simplified here for the purposes of illustration) that, from the examination of fossil remains, a theory of human evolution can be unfolded. But, as can be appreciated from the discussion so far, when considering the key features of hominids (as listed above) the fossil record does not support a simple linear progression, but instead argues for the existence of a patchwork pattern of evolution. That is, the fossil record does not provide incontrovertible evidence of a linear progression to modern humans. Indeed, the existence of interchangeability over time between gracile and robust features illustrated in the fossil record suggests a non-linear progression to modern humans. There have been many changes in direction, with gracile forms giving way to more robust species, only for gracility to reemerge in the fossil record at a later date. There are continuities over time, particularly with respect to the slow development of an upright stance and bipedalism, and increases in brain volume, but there is also evidence of an enduring mosaicism in the record. The overall norm with respect to early *Homo* seems to be away from the sequential development of distinct forms clearly separated from others, and towards an intermix of different morphological developments a different times.

The Steinheim skull from Germany which has both Neanderthal and modern characteristics, and the Caune de l'Arago remains that have features associated with both *H. erectus* and Neanderthals provide good examples of this inter-species mosaicism. The remains found in 1927 by Turville-Petre in the Wadi Amud close to Lake Galilee also fall into this category, having both modern and primitive characteristics. There are other problems in the fossil record in addition to this intermixing of morphological forms. Stringer and Gamble (1993) point out that some African fossils from 500,000 to 200,000 years ago are difficult to classify in terms of the broad fossil record. For example, a partial skull from Ndutu in Tanzania has a more modern shape in some respects than the contemporary Bodo male (Clark 1990). And from the Salé and Thomas Quarries in Morocco there have been found remains which have a combination of small brain and large teeth but otherwise have a relatively anatomically advanced morphology (Hublin 1985, 1992).

There are other examples that could be cited, but the purpose here is not to document the complete fossil record, these examples are given instead to illustrate that many current interpretations of early human evolution are based upon making the best attempt possible to provide a coherent account of a complex set of data. The question to be asked, though, is whether this is the best approach to adopt when there appears to be clear evidence of non-linear processes within human evolution? The two things that stand out clearly when considering early human evolution are: firstly, the great complexity that exists in chronological commentaries on fossil remains; and, second, in consequence of this complexity, the questions which arise with regard to attempts to provide a clear account of the early process of evolution remain largely unanswered. And when attention is turned towards a consideration of the later stages of evolution to modern humans, the picture is no less unclear.

The Emergence of Modern Humans

The events which took place from 200,000 years ago to the emergence of modern humans are less clear than even the preceding discussion of morphological adaptation. There are two basic forms of explanation for the emergence of a global modern human form. In one view there was one migration of *H. erectus* from Africa which gave rise to a western and an Asian *H. erectus*. In Europe *H. erectus* evolved into Neanderthals and then into a modern human, whereas in Asia the process took place via an archaic human from to a modern from. The opposing view argues that *H. erectus* in Asia and the Neanderthal in Europe became transplanted by a further wave of migration from Africa of modern humans around 150,000 years ago. It is argued by those holding to the second migration theory, that these modern humans arrived in Java around 60,000 years ago, and by 40,000 were displacing Neanderthals in Europe. Which of these is the case is of a central interest to this current analysis as the first view, which advocates multi-regional evolution, depicts a non-linear transition to modern humans. Conversely, the second migration hypothesis postulates a largely linear progression in which modern humans arose once in a, by implication, generally isolated population of African ancestors.

The suggestion that modern humans arose uniquely from a second wave of migration by modern humans from Africa around 150,000 years ago is in general terms a linear hypothesis. Conversely, to claim that modern humans arose from the first migration of *H. erectus* around 1.8 to one million years ago has elements of a more non-linear process. This is so because with respect to the first hypothesis, modern humans arose within a single habitat in response to unique selective pressures and then migrated throughout Asia and Europe with little transformation, where, except with respect to minor transformations in response to climate, the form has remained largely unchanged to the present day. This depicts a single strand of development with respect to central features of modern human morphology from *H. erectus* to modern Human. A multi-regional model suggests a contrary process whereby the complex mix of different forms of early humans, for example, between Neanderthal and a late *H. erectus* in west Europe, continued side by side for many generations and from which, through interbreeding, various forms of modern humans came into being. Some of these sub-species would have had a survival advantage at one time, whilst during other periods different forms persevered.

From this perspective an element of chance or unpredictability played a great part in the success or failure of a species or sub-species. The complex system of interacting types which thus arose produced unpredictable outcomes in terms of the composition of various characteristics. And by chance some won through whilst others died out. But what does the evidence tell us regarding the likelihood of one of these hypotheses being more likely than the other?

Stringer and Gamble (1993) are clear in their view that it was the second wave of emigration which provided the basis for modern global humankind. They argue that the fossil record shows a distinct sequential emergence of humankind in Africa from ancient specimens of Bodo and Broken Hill, through transitional forms to the appearance of modern humans around 1000,000 years ago in the African Middle Stone Age. Of course, as they recognise, this fossil evidence may merely point out events unfolding in Africa which also occurred elsewhere. However, they argue further that there is a lack of evidence of such an early transition in areas outside Africa. They also cite genetic evidence which, in demonstrating that amongst modern Africans there is greater genetic variation in mitochondrial DNA than outside Africa, also supports the idea that Africans were the first modern humans. Such conclusions are drawn from the fact that mitochondrial DNA is transformed solely by way of mutation, rather than by way of recombination during sexual reproduction. As the rate of mutation occurs at a known rate (established at about three percent per million years by Cann et al 1987) the degree of intra-group variation can be used to estimate a date of common origin. However, this method of dating the original modern human has recently been weakened by findings by Eyre Walker et al (1999) and Hagelberg et al (1999). Both groups have found strong evidence for the existence of genetic recombination between mitochondria, thus casting considerable doubt on previous estimates arrived at by way of mitochondrial mutation rates. rather than mitochodria provide a fixed measure of relatedness, the issue of dating by this method becomes very uncertain.

If mitochondrial evidence becomes unreliable then the focus is placed more firmly once again As has been argued, this record is far from complete and there must be strong doubts on the reliability of an approach that within which there is so much missing and problematic data. The fact that similar fossils of modern humans have not been found outside Africa does not prove that modern humans did not exist elsewhere at that time. Of course Stringer and Gamble and others do not claim that they have proved their hypothesis beyond doubt. It is clear that theirs and other similar discussions are still based on interpretation rather than an established comprehensive chronology. This interpretation may eventually prove to be be correct, but if data that is difficult to interpret is included in this analysis, data that shows discontinuities in development strands, then a different perspective can be offered. A perspective that is based upon the analysis of discontinuities rather than the seeking of continuity where it may not exist.

From looking at certain of the evidence used to support current ideas about the chronology of human origins, the fossil record appears to offer more support for complexity and mosaicism than single continuous lines of development. The data seem to suggest a non-linear pattern of evolution rather than the implied linear progression featured most often, by implication if not overtly recognised, in much current research.

Evolution by Linear or Non-linear Processes?

Before the substantive discussion of early human evolution continues it may be helpful to the reader if a brief explanation of the way the terms linear and non-linear are being used within this analysis with respect to human evolution.

In general a linear process is one in which causality can be most easily addressed as it refers to or makes use of the concept of continuous change, that is change by way of systematic and predictable stages. This is the default approach adopted in most traditional research in the biological and social sciences. These are the simple analyses that we all encounter when first approach a basic piece of research, they generally take the form: if a + b then c. Researchers generally want to find out what happens in a hypothesised causal chain of events that give rise in a direct way to an observed outcome. These approaches tend to produced findings based on correlations, for example, "if you are young and male you are at a greater risk of being involved in violent crime than someone within the general population". The literature is full of this kind of research as social and natural scientists seek to describe as accurately as they can the causes of particular outcomes. If the simple equation a + b = c does not provide a good answer, then other factors are introduced and, in more sophisticated analyses, these additional factors together with the original elements of the research are weighted against each other to find which variables in which combination contribute the most to the observed variance in the measure outcome. Now this works extremely well for generating descriptions of large populations, and useful policy-related findings can result from this approach. However, when the analysis moves from a broad picture of large groups and seeks to understand cases that do not correlate with observed large-scale effects, this approach is not effective. This is because linear approaches, studies based on the concept of continuous change, seek to reveal conformity between data and ignore both the temporal dimension (and therefore produce atemporal snapshots in time) and exceptional cases. This is a severe limitation when used with complex natural and cultural systems as these dynamic systems change over time such that patterns of interaction within such system vary discontinuously. In consequence, it can be difficult to provide a description of the state of such systems which would be valid for all time periods. For example, although it is relatively easy to produce a broad descriptive characterisation of UK weather over an annual period: it is cold in winter with temperatures often below 0 degrees C, warmer in spring, though often cloudy with rain, warmest in summer with the highest levels of sunshine, and cooler again in autumn: it is very difficult to provide a detailed forecast for more than a period of a few days. What this means is that if we try to paint with more than either a broad brush, or limit our analysis to closely defined conditions (say, the next 48 hours) our ability to described accurately patterns of change diminishes. The reason for this is that weather systems are non-linear; they change in a discontinuous way. That is, the configuration of determining elements (our previous a + b + ...) changes over time and, in not being unchanging as in linear models, precise outcomes cannot be predicted. Changes in non-linear systems arise as a consequence of all the interactions taking place within the system, so in this sense outcomes can be seen to be an emergent property of the system. Compound interactions take place in such systems such that the overall configuration of the system at any given moment in time varies. The state of the system at any given time is thus an emergent outcome of the sum of interactions. The system thus evolves as an outcome of great interconnectivity between all the comprising elements. The constant shifting means that there can be no great certainty about any given empirical state during the evolution of the system. We can gain knowledge about the identity of the elements, and we can note emergent outcomes as they arise, but we cannot tell exactly what will happen within the system for one moment to the next. This also means that it is not possible to re-trace the originating state of a given emergent outcome. Empirically, it will not be possible to discover the specific configuration of the system that gave rise to any particular emergent outcome. What actually happens to a system is a chance outcome based on a certain configuration of elements, the nature of which cannot be known retrospectively. These systems are dynamical, nonlinear and discontinuous, not atemporal, linear and continuous. The concepts of emergence and interconnectiveness are key aspects of complexity theory, and may assist in our understanding of the process of human evolution in that they may define certain limitations of current approaches.

So, having engaged in this aside, how does an appreciation of the differences in linear and non-linear systems help our understanding of human evolution? Well, in terms of early human evolution, it leads to questioning whether we have enough data to establish whether or not *H. erectus* evolved in a single environment in Africa or from intermixing between existing hominid species. The fossil evidence suggests a mosaical pattern of change rather one within which change from one ancestral type to another occurred in a distinct and unambiguous manner. This suggests that at a given time in human evolutionary history there existed side-by side different variations of human ancestors that could, perhaps, reasonably be assumed to interbreed. This means that, in considering this from the perspective of complexity theory where outcomes arise from interconnectiveness between dissimilar elements, it becomes possible to included in considerations of human evolution the possibility of complexity in the fossil record being due to discontinuous evolution. Where previously linear analyses may have been the default pattern of reasoning about lines of evolution, reference to the study of the characteristics of non-linear systems and complexity theory suggests other that other approaches may be necessary. Being presented with two paradigms of analysis means that new questions need to be asked. If a linear progression is likely then there needs to be identified fossil evidence that provides a conclusive uninterrupted chronology of human evolution linked to known environmental conditions. If this cannot be obtained then new ways of viewing this problem must be considered.

This last point concerning environmental conditions presents a particular problem because it is extremely difficult to provide a suitable description of an environment which would lead to the selection of the, arguably, four major explicit characteristics that form the basis for depicting a species as the first *Homo*. These four features are: firstly, there has to be present a morphology adapted towards bipedalism in terms of hip and pelvic structure and the positioning of the cranium. Second, the skull and brain has to have undergone significant enlargement. Third, the vocal tract will have to have adapted to vocalisation. And, lastly, there would have to have occurred adaptations to the upper limb which facilitated greater manual dexterity. Of course there are other adaptations involved in classifying a species as early Homo, but even limiting the list to these four features illustrates the problem associated with assuming that these arose in a single environment. And this task becomes even more difficult if evolution took place, as fossil evidence cited above suggests, in a mosaic or patchwork pattern rather than by linear accretion. If this is so, then it begins to seem very unlikely that any single set of environmental conditions could engender such changes. This complexity in human evolution is problematic because unless a pattern can be discerned in the evolution of early humans any simple application of Darwinian natural selection becomes difficult to sustain. Although we need to know why the earliest hominids stood up, why changes to the upper limb took place, why they developed larger brains and why these broad trends continued and led to the appearance of modern humans, if patterns cannot be identified then the project becomes almost intractable.

Selecting for Humankind

There have been many attempts to identify the environmental circumstances of this early stage of human evolution, but none has gained full acceptance within the scientific community. During the 1960s and later the most current explanation of the emergence of humans was based on the savannah model. It was generally believed that the human lineage stemmed from climatic changes which reduced forest habitat and increased dry, open grassland. According to Susman (1987), all theories of human origins in the previous 30 years had argued for the importance of territoriality, meat-eating and social organisation within the context of a savannah habitat. Such research continued in the 1990s when Wheeler (1991a, 1991b) again produced analyses of savannah-led human evolution. In fact many writers have argued that the dry African savannah is the most likely environment from which we stemmed. Descriptions of the need to scout for predators or prey (supposedly easier for a species which stands on two legs), reduce the impact of the sun (standing up gives rise to a smaller surface area impacted on by the suns rays) and the needs of a tool making and weapon throwing species have all found their way into the general debate. But despite attracting support (or did they enter that mystical realm of knowledge where acceptance occurs from the absence of convincing alternatives) there is little real evidence that these circumstances provided the crucial vector in the evolution of modern humans. So, even after over 30 years of attention on the savannah as a starting point for human evolution, little progress has been made because every argument put forward can easily be refuted by a counter claim, or by revealing inherent weaknesses. For example, if bipedalism arose for thermoregulatory purposes, as claimed by Wheeler (1991a), surely it would be likely that many other species inhabiting hot, dry climates would have adapted in the same way. Indeed the fossil record is full of examples of divergent evolution, so why not in this case? As Dennett (1995) has pointed out there are "good moves" in evolutionary design space that are found independently throughout the living world. If events were as continuous as Wheeler and others have suggested by implication, then surely other species would also be walking around on two legs; if it was a good idea for our ancestors, then why not for other species as well? Overall, it would appear that there has been little progress in this area, and it would seem that anthropologists are no closer to being able to describe the environmental circumstances of our origins then they were 20 or 30 years ago. Even more recent attempts to redefine savannah as a mixed environment of forests, woodlands and open grasslands have not changed the basic characteristics of the model, with the central focus still being sentinel behaviour and thermoregulation (Morgan 1997). This latest reformulation also still has the problem of describing how these circumstances gave rise to morphological characteristics unique to humans when many other primates would have shared such a habitat.

The idea that evolution took place in one location implies that change took place by way of a continuous process. It is a simple Darwinian perspective; the environment changes so the species adapts. So, if this is to work for human evolution then our distant last common ancestor would have to have been subjected to an environment unique for a primate, and not a forest/grassland habitat favoured by other primates. Now despite the obviousness of this stance as an analytical device there is only one writer (to my knowledge) who has risen to the task of pursuing this approach and produced a detailed discussion of the most likely habitat. Starting in 1982 with the publication of her first book on the subject, Elaine Morgan has pursued an analysis of human origins which argues that the originating habitat was not a dry savannah but instead an isolated African lake. Whether or not her findings prove eventually to be the best current attempt to define the environment of human emergence, and some important misgivings stemming from this current analysis will be considered below, her work is worth citing as an example of one attempt at producing a comprehensive description of the relationship between morphology and environment.

Morgan (1982, 1990, 1997) contends that the existing fossil record is consistent with the proposition that around six to eight million years ago at the northern end of the Rift Valley a group of early hominids dwelt in a water environment and adapted to an aquatic existence. Over time their descendants migrated south along rivers and waterways, where later fossil remains have been found. This adaptation to an aquatic environment was only partial as the time span was limited to a period of only two or three million years (compared to the 70 million years of wales and dolphins and 25 to 30 million years for seals). It was, argues Morgan, this ancient aquatic environment that provided the basis for key aspects of human morphology to arise. Bipedalism, hairlessness, the presence of relatively large amounts of subcutaneous fat, adaptations to the larynx which facilitated breathing through the mouth are all interestingly and persuasively linked to the demands of a hypothetical aquatic environment. It is not my intention to review the strengths and weaknesses of Morgan's work, she does this quite adequately herself, but rather to allow these brief references to her conclusions to illustrate the requirements of any theorising about the environmental circumstances of the last common ancestor between ourselves and other apes. What Morgan has done, whether to everyone's satisfaction or not, is to attempt to meet the challenge of a belief in a continuous evolutionary path and described the facilitating environment.

In terms of the scope of characteristics considered, Morgan's work is of interest to those concerned to establish the nature of the environmental circumstances of the last common ancestor. Her work has attracted heavy criticism from many established scholars but it is difficult to refute, as Dennett (1995) has noted (he remarks that although her work has not found favour amongst anthropologists it has not generally been refuted). In terms of considering the contribution that complexity theory may bring to human origins research its greatest weakness is in providing yet another analysis based on the concept of continuous change; one in which a single cause is held to give rise directly to a variety of complex outcomes. If the few strands of doubt presented here are put together then attention should be focused instead on the existence of a complex path of evolution within which morphological characteristics are seen to be the emergent outcome of great interconnectiveness between component elements. One in which different kinds of early humans with differentiated morphological characteristics, that have arisen in consequence of exposure to differing environmental conditions, came together and interbred. That is, multi-regional morphological development within a migratory (nomadic) species that continued to re-mix over varying periods of time. An ebb and flow of movement, change and cross-breeding. A complex system within which modern humans emerged as a consequence of chance events in the evolutionary past.

Beyond the Environmental and Morphological Correlation

These early comments on human evolution from a complex perspective provide an important basis for what is to come in this current analysis, but as yet nothing has been said about the most important characteristic of modern humans, our remarkable cognitive abilities. Providing insights into the some of the earliest adaptations to a modern human form, such as bipedalism, it contributes only indirectly to our understanding of the most important feature of modern humans, our symbolic reasoning ability and our use of language. And in turning attention to the evolution of language it is necessary to move forward in evolutionary time. Although it is possible to detect a progressive emergence of the modern human form over the last three million years (Tobias 1994), a progressive large-scale enlargement of the brain first arose only about two million years ago, with the appearance of *H.habilis* (some four million years after the emergence of the hominids). So to be able to interpret this most important phase of human evolution it will be necessary to consider circumstances other than the broad habitat occupied by hominids over the last two million years. And in doing so, comment on whether linear progress be ascertained, or whether non-linear events are depicted.

Cranial Expansion and the Emergence of Modern Humans

The consideration of the early environment within which important changes in early human morphology took place is an important component of this current book, but, as was made clear in the above discussion, that discussion relates to periods much older than the two millions years or so during which it is recognised that species of *Homo* experienced large-scale enlargement of the brain. In consequence that broad body of work can offer only limited insights into the the emergence of a large and morphologically complex brain, and the subsequent acquisition of language and symbolic reasoning.

Increasingly, the role of culture has been identified as an important element in human evolution, particularly with regard to language acquisition and the development of symbolic reasoning. From this perspective it is argued that it is probably the case that part of the process of human evolution has been determined by changes to the environment affected by humans themselves. An environment so changed would give rise to a variation in selective pressures which would in turn engender further adaptation by way of natural selection. And it may even be the case that at some stage in human evolution it was an emerging social life which provided the selective environment, as argued by Knight (1991) in his depiction of female control over reproduction being the basis of the development of culture. Clearly, the role of human manipulation of the environment and the demands of a emerging social life cannot be ignored. Hence the problem of the emergence of self-conscious awareness and the genesis of social life and will be the subject of chapter two. Firstly, however, the preceding discussion should be drawn to some preliminary conclusions.

Towards a Complex Perspective on the Emergence Humankind

Firstly, in above discussion has drawn attention to the fact that the fossil record provides evidence for a mosaicism in development such that arguments for ideas about the importance of interconnectivity and emergence within human evolution can be put forward. Although the trend in human origins research has been towards seeking a last common ancestor, identifying an engendering environment and provided a linear account of the fossil record there is evidence that such a task may be difficult if not impossible to complete. Many natural systems display characteristics of non-linearity which are a feature of dynamic change over time. Such systems often feature unpredictability and discontinuities rather than predictable evolution. It has been argued that the fossil record reveals discontinuities such that claims for a complex pattern of evolution can be made. That human evolution rather than occurring in one place at one time was instead the result of complex patterns of migration and interbreeding between different lines. If this was the case then there would be no "missing link" between human and other ape evolutionary lines, but instead a complex mosaic of change which eventually gave rise to modern humans. The case for this approach is further supported when it is recognised that humankind has become an agent of its own evolution to a greater extent than any other species. The resultant expanded network of interconnectivity would add even further levels of complexity and new patterns of emergence.

As the previous discussion has illustrated, in analyses of early human evolution attention has been focused to a large degree on the selective pressure of non-human aspects of the environment. That is, for example, to concentrate analyses of human origins on the behavioural demands of a hunter-gatherer existence, or the physical requirements of using primitive tools. Or, conversely, to centre on the climatic pressures of dwelling on, say, a dry Savannah, as is widely claimed. These approaches centre on the physical world in that they draw attention to aspects of the non-cultural or non-social world from which adaptive changes take place in the human form or in human behaviour. Increasingly, however, such approaches are being combined with perspectives which feature the impact on evolution of intentional and social behaviour on the part of humans and their distant forebears.

Taken together, such analyses do not only address issues relating to human physical form, but also include interests relating to human consciousness. Studies in evolutionary psychology and neuroscience have produced results in recent years which have provided significant new insights into the way mind is firmly grounded in a brain which is, in turn, the outcome of adaptation. From such work it is argued increasingly that even aspects of our self-conscious self have arisen adaptively both historically and during lived experiences. For example, Edelman (1992) has produced a Darwinian account of the contemporary formation of aspects of conscious awareness.

From environmentally and socially grounded studies a wealth of knowledge concerning the origins of humankind has arisen. The processes of reverse engineering have provided many new insights into the possible circumstances of humankind's emergence. However, despite many years of human origins research there has not yet arisen an agreed set of circumstances from which humankind emerged as a consciously aware bipedal hominid. There is as yet no identifiable last common ancestor between humankind and other apes. Nor is there agreement on whether key events in the evolution of modern humans took place on a single occasion in Africa some between 200,000 and 100,000 years ago, or separately in many distinct places around the world, or on the banks of an isolated lake somewhere in Africa.

Analyses which underpin either the second migrational or multi-regional approach have provided imaginative and skilful insights into the beginnings of modern humankind. None, however, have as yet established the veracity of their ideas beyond reasonable doubt, and so they should be considered only as working hypotheses. Especially, as illustrated in the above discussion, given that the evidence may otherwise indicate a complex interplay of divergence, convergence, migration and homology as much as it does a linear process of adaptation in response to a specific environment.

This last statement may seem rather obvious to the reader when first encountered. After all, it could be argued, it is just the case as yet that there has not been enough research carried out to establish once and for all where humankind came from, in terms of the development of specific characteristics. It could be argued that the problem lies not with current approaches, but with a lack of data. Therefore, some time in the future there will have been collected another fossil, or groups of fossils, which will prove beyond reasonable doubt where humankind fits in the fossil record, from what geological period, environmental conditions and behavioural context it stemmed and the rest will be worked out quite easily. From matching the changes in our physical shape with known environmental and deduced behavioural changes there will emerge a synchronised picture of human evolution by adaptive response. We will be able to see most of the whole picture.

Of course, in practice, this would not really be possible, even if the data described above became available. From whatever starting position the analysis began, at some point it would have to be established why this changed with respect to the human ancestor and not others? After all, we are not the only tool using species. For example, chimpanzees are known to use sticks to collect insects. The only reasonable answer to this would have to be, to return once again to this point, that our ancestors experienced an environment different from that of any other primate. This is unlikely, or at least less likely then the counter view presented here, that early humans engaged in nomadic behaviour and experienced a variety of environments, and that from this there emerged a set of morphological characteristics different from any other contemporary primate. From this environmental and morphological diversity there emerged a way of life within which a fundamental symbolic reasoning and language ability imparted an advantage in food gathering, defence (against hostile organisms or aspects of the climate) or reproduction. Once this process began, it would then alter significantly humankind's engagement with the environment. As a considerable body of new research has argued, analyses need to move beyond merely relating morphological change to given environmental conditions, and look at the effect humankind itself has had on the environment, and thus its own evolution. At some unknowable point in our past feedback between the environment and human behaviour began to drive further evolution. In consequence the founding circumstances of human evolution expanded to include the emergence of a cultural context to human existence.

This focus has been reflected in the works of Dawkins (1976, 1982), Knight (1991), Odling-Smee (1994) and Premack and Premack (1994), to name but a few. What these writers have in common is a perspective which argues for an interaction between genes and culture in setting the context for human evolution. Although genetic inheritance may be the mechanism through which adaptive traits are passed on from one generation to the next, human culture contributes directly to this process through changing the environment from which selective pressures emerge. Work by Durham (1991) provides a good illustration of co-evolution by way of culture and genetic interaction. This work focused on an analysis of the Kwa speaking people of West Africa who had developed agricultural practices that provided good breeding conditions for malarial carrying mosquitoes. In consequence, through natural selection, these people gained increased resistance to malaria. However, there was an unfortunate side effect to this adaptation as those who were homozygous for the anti-malarial gene developed sickle-cell anaemia. Interestingly, Livingstone (1958) argued that the anti-malarial gene persisted in the population as in the heterozygous state due to the resultant partial protection against malaria. However, it is hard to imagine the circumstances where once a genetic change that is either fatal or significantly detrimental to well-being has taken place, it will disappear from a population without further selective pressure. On the contrary there is no established mechanism for systematic genetic change except by way of natural selection and change by continuous modification; notwithstanding claims for a probable mutation effect, or genetic entropy, (Brace 1963) or punctuated equilibria (Gould and Eldredge 1993). The only way sickle-cell anaemia could disappear from the descendants of the founding Kwa agricultural population would be either by genetic screening which could forestall the occurrence of homozygosity, or if an environment or habitat arose within which heterozygosity had detrimental outcomes. Such a habitat may arise through non-human causes or by way of human action.

Clearly, what is being argued here is that although evolution takes place through genetic alteration by way of natural selection, the genesis of those environmental changes can occur by way of human cultural activities. That is, the process is not linear, but instead involves feedback between the environment and humankind. Indeed, this is only the beginning of the complexity involved as human cultural activities not only change the external non-human environment, but also work internally within human societies to change modes of reproduction and food gathering, which then impact further on the external environment. Human evolution has thus proceeded not only genetically but also, increasingly, culturally. We not only inherit genes but also environments and knowledge about those environments (Premack and Premack 1994). There is thus a nested complexity where feedback from different levels results in phenotypic adaptation. Hence what is needed is an orientation to the study of human origins and evolution which accounts for the emergence of humankind by way of a non-linear, nature-culture complex.

However, notwithstanding the likelihood of the actions of early *Homo* being in part a determinant in human evolution, there still remains a need to identify, theoretically if not empirically through fossil or geological data, the circumstances from which modern humans, and some early ancestors, first gained the ability to reason symbolically and acquire language. If co-evolution between nature and culture is the key to understanding the evolutionary progress of Homo, then it is important to reflect on the evolutionary path of our cognitive abilities so that the substance of human mental life can be unfolded and the manner of our engagement with the natural world described more fully.

2 The Emergence of Symbolic Reasoning

Despite the importance of the evolution of bipedalism, reduced jaw line, fore limb adaptations and other broad morphological characteristics which establish *homo sapiens* as a distinct primate species, by far the most important evolutionary outcome is the manifestation of symbolic reasoning. That is, the facility to reason abstractly in terms of past and future events and not merely have cognition of the present. This ability to reason symbolically has also given rise to spoken languages as a means of communication. Although other species use vocal means of communication, only humankind has grammatically structured languages. By way of the use of language, humankind has established cultures comprising vast accumulations of knowledge, manufacturing skills and techniques, art and music. No other species has attained the quality of communication through succeeding generations that humankind has through the existence of complex languages. Although information about exploiting a habitat can be passed on by social animals such as bees, ants and termites, this takes place almost solely by the genetic inheritance of behavioural traits. And even social species much closer to humankind, such as chimpanzees, are limited in their ability to preserve skills and knowledge from one generation to the next. Although learning a repertoire of behaviours which assist survival clearly play a part in chimpanzee maturation processes, these are extremely limited in terms of innovation from one generation to another. Humankind, it would seem, is unique in being able to gain abstract understanding of the external world and communicate such knowledge accurately and reliably to others. This, then, is the great mystery of humankind, although it is relatively easy to speculate on why humankind stood up on two legs and stayed that way, or why our forelimbs adapted such that the hand became able to grasp and manipulate objects with greater dexterity than other species, it is less easy to discern the extraordinary process through which the ability to compose symphony music come into being? Clearly there are collective moments in this process as, unlike other human adaptations, language is only meaningful if it is shared. Being able to pick up a stone and fashion a tool may be of use to a single ancestor, but being able to communicate complex ideas would be purposeless unless it was experienced collectively. Hence a focus on collective enterprises must be at the centre of any reflection on or investigation into the beginnings of symbolic thought and the use of language. In addressing these issues it will be necessary to consider what it was about early human behaviour which laid the ground for the emergence of language.

As with other adaptations, the circumstances of early human life must have been qualitatively different for symbolic reasoning and language to have evolved only with respect to *Homo* and no other species. And it will be necessary to speculate on these circumstances if progress is to be made in unfolding the path to sentience. However, the problem is more complex regarding symbolic reasoning and language than with respect to other adaptations, as human reasoning is dependent upon the existence of a brain within which symbolic mentation can take place. Without there being adaptations to the brain, human language could not have arisen. So the process of change to the human brain which made symbolic reasoning possible must have began before a language emerged. But how could this have taken place from a Darwinian perspective? Before language existed proficiency in complex symbolic communication could not have been a selective pressure. So language itself could not have given rise to brain adaptations which led to symbolic mentation. Changes which facilitated the development of language must, surely, have taken place prior to the emergence of language. Now, in Darwinian terms this is problematic as there can be no changes in morphology that can arise adaptively with respect to a given trait prior to that trait emerging. It is the old chicken and the egg problem. There cannot be language without certain morphological changes to the brain having taken place, but it would seem that from this simple basis these changes cannot occur until they are selected for by language use. Clearly there is a dilemma here which must be unravelled before progress can be made.

When faced with such dilemmas in evolution some authors have referred to the existence of so-called preadaptations. A preadaptation is held to be a change in form which takes place in an organism prior to the final use being achieved. For example, the elongation of a giraffes neck commenced prior to the eating advantage being achieved. However, once the survival or reproduction rates of those giraffes with slightly extended necks improved over any non-preadapted members, then selective pressure led to further extended necks. In terms of the present concern with the enlargement of human brains the argument would be that increased brain size was preadaptive, but once increased mentation and manual skills emerged brain size became adaptive. As the reader will readily appreciate, there are considerable problems with this approach. Darwinian evolution can only occur with respect to the direct selection of distinct traits or characteristics, there cannot be anticipation on the part of an organism of something that may be of use in uncounted generations time. A belief in preadaptation implies that an organism can guess the future. Such ideas invoke either a higher power leading biological development, or a homunculus sitting somewhere inside the organism interpreting events. All such approaches do is shift the analysis to another level. Faced with only this possibility we would either need to give up science for religion, or discover the cause and effect of a homunculus (in effect, an internal, independent entity which carries out a required function).

Of course there is no need for a homunculus as Darwin's theory of evolution by natural selection provides a far better basis for understanding adaptation than theories such as preadaptation. And, although spiritual knowledge is an important and considerably valuable aspect of human life, science too has a role in human affairs so we should not completely abandon rigorous scientific reflection until we have exhausted our analytic abilities. So imagining that the brain spontaneously or by external or other forces began to enlarge outwith an adaptive advantage is unhelpful in the task of unravelling our evolutionary past.

It would seem from the above that it is unlikely that the brain could have evolved at all. The problem can be presented quite simply. For the brain to have adapted sufficiently to be the basis for the emergence of symbolic reasoning and language there must have been prior development, as symbolic reasoning and language could not be the basis of their own emergence. As Dennett (1995) has pointed out so expertly, there are no "sky hooks" which act outwith Darwinian processes to redesign species. That is, the standard Darwinian position is that there are no processes outside natural selection that we need consider when viewing adaptive change. But if this is so then we come back to the chicken and the egg. The evolution of the brain cannot have taken place. Well this is true only if the changes in brain size which began for *Homo* some two million years ago were at that time related to symbolic reasoning and language. However, if such changes took place for reasons other than from the selective pressure of symbolic reasoning and language then the dilemma is avoided. Now it may seem that what is being invoked once again is preadaptation, which is clearly not a feasible proposition, but this need not be the case as it is within the bounds of Darwinian evolution theory to accept that new traits and characteristics can arise from changes to previous adaptations. Hence it may be that the human brain increased in size for reasons unrelated to symbolic thought, but once having gained in size and complexity, symbolic thought emerged. This in turn paved the way for language, and, once acquired in this way, the selective advantage imparted led to further selection and subsequent evolution in both the complexity and range of mentation. In effect the increase in brain size which began some two million years ago could have occurred by way of changes in specific characteristics for reasons initially unrelated to abstract thought. Gould and Vrba (1982) considered this form of change to be what he termed "exaptations", by which he meant, to use Dennett's (1995) definition, the exploitation of something previously undesigned. That is, something which prior to being adapted to present use, arose as an undirected consequence of some other development. This definition is important as it means that the prior development of changes in form which become ultimately adaptive could occur initially by way of non-Darwinian change. In the case of the brain, this would mean that the precondition of cerebral enlargement did not arise adaptively by way of natural selection, but instead as a chance off-shoot of some other process. What exaptation implies is a reliance in human evolution on rapid random change unrelated to any previous stage of development. Of course there would have to be a cause of the shift towards a larger brain, but this need not have been anything to do with symbolic reasoning or language. This may seem problematic but such ideas are a central feature of complexity theory. Recall from chapter one that the status of a dynamic nonlinear system arises as a product of the great interconnectiveness that exists between elements that comprise the system. The state of the system is at any moment an emergent outcome of all the connections within the system. Or, in other words, an outcome is a resolution of the system a one moment in time. This means that outcomes do not have a conventional statistical probability, any particular outcome is always highly improbable (think about the problem of calculating the probability of your life turning out just the way it is at this exact moment). In this sense exaptations are emergent outcomes. Of course an exaptation still needs to be adaptive, the difference is that such outcomes have not arisen in a continuous manner with respect to the target characteristic.

The concept of exaptations has received a considerable amount of criticism from Dennet, Dawkins and others, generally because those subscribing to this theory have not provided an adequate explanation of how this process unfolds in the natural world. Gould and Lewontin

(1979) attempted to argue for the existence of exaptations by way of an analysis of the formation of spandrels in constructing domes on rounded arches. Spandrels are the tapered triangular spaces which arise from the intersection of two rounded arches which meet at a right angle. Gould and Lewontin (1979) argue that the spandrels themselves did not arise directly by way of an intentional design selected aesthetically by the architect, but as an unintended outcome of placing a dome on rounded arches. Only after they appeared did spandrels become used for inventive decorational purposes. A spandrel thus arose not by way of selection for aesthetic reasons, but via exaptation by virtue of design limitations . Once a dome resting on arches has been specified, spandrels must come into existence. Once they have emerged in this way they can then be adapted to other uses. This line of reasoning has been very successful in terms of propagation, but Dennett (1995), has shown that a spandrel is not the only possible solution to this architectural problem. As Dennett (1995) points out, spandrels were (and still are) selected because they are approximately the minimal surface area possible for solving the design problem, and, secondly, they can be used aesthetically for decorative purposes. The attempt by Gould and Lewontin to ground ideas about exaptations are thus somewhat weakened. However, notwithstanding these interesting critiques of Gould's and Lewontin's concept, when the notion of an exaptation is reworked in line with ideas from complexity theory, this may yet provide a way of unfolding the evolutionary path of elaborate traits such as symbolic reasoning, for which a path of continuous development is difficult to construct.

However, even though exaptation may lie somewhere along the pathway to symbolic reasoning it is still necessary to seek out the adaptive moments that gave rise to the initial gradual increase in the size and complexity of the human brain. Given that these changes may well have been initiated through the development of traits other than that of language use, attention needs to be focused on the antecedents to increased cranial capacity prior to the emergence of symbolic reasoning. This is a complex task and any definitive solution may be beyond any contemporary analysis, however recent research on Darwinian explanations of brain development have provided important new insights.

The Adaptation of the Human Brain

Terrance Deacon has recently brought out a book on the co-evolution of language and the human brain which may prove as important to understanding the evolution of symbolic reasoning and language as has Edelman's work. Deacon (1997) argues that the human brain has not evolved a distinct grammatical ability which is universal across humankind. Instead there has evolved side-by-side an ability to reason symbolically and a vocalised language. People learn to speak languages easily, he contends, not because they have some form of in-built language instinct, but because language has evolved alongside human cognitive evolution. Children learn languages easily because the languages we have are selected for by the need for children to learn them easily. Any language which was difficult to learn because it mapped poorly with human cognitive ability could not be selected. And conversely, being relatively skilled at an emerging vocal language would also be adaptive. Hence, forms of language and the facility to employ language socially co-evolved.

If this is so, and Deacon's analysis is a convincing use of Darwinian evolutionary theory to explain the evolution of language, then it implies that an ability to reason symbolically must have preceded the emergence of language. This seems the most simple possible chain of events. Some ability to reason symbolically arose, this led to attempts at gestured and perhaps verbalised communication which were tried and tested in practice until selective pressures led to the successful propagation of certain forms, which then formed the template for further adaptations in language ability. This became an iterative process as further changes occurred by way of co-evolution. So, it is being argued that at some point in human evolution a hominid ancestor acquired the ability to reason in abstract terms. In thus moving on from merely denoting items and events in the way that many animals do in identifying food or predators, to being able to group these according to abstract principles, there arose an ability to symbolise the world. Once symbolic reasoning arose the potential to refer to the world beyond a merely concurrent event emerged. And being biologically a collective species, for humankind this would have led to the emergence of a communal language as abstract constructions of the external world were shared. The vocalisation of this language system would have had precedence over other forms of communication, such as signing, as its use would not compete with the manipulative function of hands or limbs. The ability to engage intentionally in complex vocalisations would have been strongly adaptive. First came symbolic thought, and later spoken languages.

The circumstances of the transition to abstract thought and language will be considered in more detail later in chapter three. First, however, it is necessary for this current discussion of the genesis of enlarged brains to move evolutionarily further back rather than forwards into language and culture. The discussion has referred to the emergence of language and symbolic reasoning to illustrate that the analysis presented here, implies that an ability to think symbolically arose prior to the acquisition of language, so, by implication the enlargement of the brain (particularly with respect to encephalisation - an increase in the brain/body ratio) could not have occurred through language-related selective pressure but must instead have been associated with other forms of symbolic thought. But, once again there is a paradox in assuming that this other form of symbolic reasoning gave rise to developments to the brain which were the foundation of its own emergence. It would seem that encephalisation must have occurred prior to the onset of symbolic reasoning, and Darwinian evolutionary theory states that this change must have occurred by way of natural selection. So the question is, what processes led to the selection of bigger brains?

Many writers have suggested that social pressure, tool making, habitat factors and many other vectors, in addition to language and abstract thought, led to the selection of greater brain size. The problem with all of these suggests and theories is that they still face the same paradox. You cannot have one without the other. What is needed is a theory of brain size increase which depicts incremental growth by way of Darwinian evolution by means other than selection for a trait which at the outset did not exist. This a a difficult condition to meet, and it may well be that we will never fully understand the processes involved but some interesting speculation by Deacon (1997) and previously discussed fossil evidence may provide some further insights. Firstly, though, it is necessary to introduce the idea of competition and selection at the neuronal level. To facilitate this process a brief overview of the work of the neuroscientists Gerald Edelman will follow before returning to Deacon's work.

One of the key concepts to be grasped in understanding Darwinian approaches to the development of the brain is the idea of neuronal selection. As with any other natural system, Darwinian perspectives on brain development hold that competition between differentiated lines of descent lead to selection. Those with characteristics more closely matched to the demands of the environment will succeed at the expense of less closely matched attributes. Edelman (1989, 1992) has formed an analysis of this type that argues for neuronal selection at three distinct levels of brain development. At the first level, termed primary repertoires, specific regions of neuronal cells form from topobiological competition between individual cell lines. Thus, although there are species level constraints on brain anatomy, neuronal network diversity is formed on an inter-species basis. At the next level, secondary repertoires are formed by way of synaptic selection. Through engagement with an external environment some synaptic pathways are reinforced through utilisation whereas others are not. Those that are utilised, or selected for, propagate at the expense of those unused. Hence those synaptic connections which best represent the demands of the environment will be selected over those which are either less fit or inappropriate. Edelman (1992) has argued that in practice both these processes will overlap developmentally. In consequence, it can be seen that diversity in brain morphology derives directly from adaptive processes at the levels of both cellular propagation and early neuronal pathway formation. In the third and most complex stage of brain development Edelman contends that primary and secondary repertoires act as the foundation from which neuronal maps are formed. These maps arise from both parallel and reciprocal connections. Each map has a distinct function to fulfil (associated with, say, orientation or colour), but each is also linked by further parallel and reciprocal connections to other maps. Through what Edelman terms reentrant signalling, separate maps are interconnected. Consequently if one map is selected for on the basis of a given function then other maps that are closely inter-linked will also be selected. From this level, different events can be linked to produce a cognitive or behavioural outcome. For example, a simple avoidance reaction in response to the perception of the trajectory of a moving object leads to a behavioural act (if someone throws a rock at your head you duck). But the inter-connectiveness described by Edelman does not stop at this level. He also outlines what he terms global maps, to describe the outcome of further reentrant connections between groups of maps. Through these means Edelman describes a process which may form the basis of building up new connections between events as new global maps are formed in response to environmental events.

This is a rather brief summary of an extremely detailed analysis, but even so it draws attention to the possible role of selection in brain development. Rather than being the result of a blueprint laid down thousands or hundreds of thousands of years ago, this analysis describes a process of development within which stochastic routines and adaptive responses to the environment also underlie the development of a modern human brain. What this also means is that the development processes of each individual brain is different, even those of identical twins. What you may perceive as red could be different from the red that others see. In fact there is probably infinite variety in the way in which individual people perceive and value external events such as music or art. Although there will be species-level constraints on outcomes (for example, not everything that could occur in the universe with respect to the perception of sound can arise for human beings), and also cultural level differences in exposure to certain environments, diversity in subjective appraisal will be the norm.

Edelman's ideas regarding the formation of neuronal pathways and networks are an important contribution to understanding brain development and the formation of cognition from a Darwinian perspective. His work shows how the mind emerges from the brain by way of natural selection. That is, how primary and secondary repertoires form the basis of neuronal maps and thus link psychology with physiology (and how as a result uncertainty of outcome is always a part of human mentation).

So, from Edelman's work it can be seen that processes of brain growth involving the generation of primary and secondary repertoires (neuronal networks and synaptic connections) arise from cellular competition and selection during development. Deacon (1997) also describes a similar process of competition through what he terms "displacement". During displacement increases in the size of certain neuronal populations leads to greater competitiveness in recruiting neuronal connections. So, if a given region of the brain increases in size relative to other regions of the brain the enlarged region becomes more successful in competing for the development of interconnections with other parts of the brain. So, if certain regions of the brain enlarge they can gain increased neuronal function by attracting greater inter-connectiveness. Now this may lead to an enhanced ability in an established area, such as colour perception, or it may initiate the development of new abilities. Recall that Edelman's work depicts what he terms the reentrant interconnections of neural maps to form global maps. Now global maps are over-arching neuronal networks which categorise maps of the external world associated with, for example, orientation or colour perception. Thus these global maps serve as the basis for higher order cognitive processes. Hence, an increase in the relative size of a specific region of the brain could, by being a location for the further emergence of global maps by way of synaptic competition or displacement, be a site for the formation of higher-order cognitive functions. Indeed, Edelman (1992) argues that, ultimately, interconnections between the limbic-brain stem (associated with arousal, pain, sleep and other similar functions) and the thalamocortical system through the proliferation of reentrant connections gave rise to higher-order perceptual responses and primary consciousness (a knowing engagement with the world through past events - see chapter four). So, if some parts of the brain increase in size relative to others, then processes of competition and selection can give rise to neuronal developments from which a primary consciousness can form. But how do brain regions get relatively larger?

So far, reference has been made to the relative increases in size of specific brain regions. The purpose of choosing this focus was to draw attention to the possibility of increased neuronal competition leading to the emergence of new cognitive functions, but an increase in relative size is only one way that new functions may arise by way of new neuronal connections. As Deacon (1997) has argued, if existing inputs to a brain region are reduced from one region then, through competition, inputs from another region can increase. Imagine that there is a region of the brain that can take only ten neural inputs. In usual circumstances it receives all ten from external sensory inputs that can be designated inputs "A", and so cannot receive any from any other source. Now in the course of evolution the number of sensory inputs "A" is reduced to only two. There is now a spare capacity in this region which can be taken up by new inputs "B" and "C". These new inputs are reentrant connections from neural maps associated with different sensory inputs from inputs "A" and hence a new neural function can develop. This is, of course, very simplistic but it does draw attention to the possibility of changes in neural and cognitive capacity which are not dependent upon initial gross changes in brain size. It is an easy step from this position to perceive that if any new functions had an adaptive advantage then they would be further enhanced by way of natural selection. So perhaps what is needed is a theory of brain evolution which depicts as the first change an increase in neuronal competition.

Deacon (1997) points out that the growth processes that lead to the human brain are different from those of a normal primate in that the outcome is a brain larger than would normally be expected of an primate our size. Whilst the growth of the body is typical of a large chimp, the brain is that of a gigantic ape. This leads him to ponder on the outcome of placing an atypically large brain in a normal sized primate body. Or more specifically, placing genotype of the brain of *Gigantopithecus* embryo (an extinct eight foot ape) into a chimpanzee embryo. He argues that the outcome would be, as the reader may suspect from the above discussion, a radical change in competitive neuronal connectivity. As the chimpanzee body would only be a fraction of the size of *Gigantopithecus*, neural projections from peripheral organs (such as, for example the eye) would be significantly reduced. The overall disproportion in brain and body size would result in changes to numerous regions and functions, some being reduced and others enlarged (Deacon 1998). Overall, the reduced input and output demands from peripheral systems would mean that those neural networks outwith these systems would develop new input and output connections relating to other functions. A larger brain than necessary to achieve normative peripheral sensory functions, would mean that peripheral neural inputs and outputs to target regions would be less than existing capacity. In consequence, interconnections which would normally lose out in competition with peripheral connections would gain new neural territory and give rise to new functions. That is, the spare capacity would be taken up by interconnections with other functions.

As speculative as these ideas may be, they do cast an interesting light on the the possible consequences of humankind having, as it does, a brain which is larger than its physical size demands. As Deacon (1997) has noted, the pattern of human brain growth is that of an immense ape whilst the body growth pattern is only that of a large chimpanzee, and, in consequence, during development new neural functions may historically have arisen. This increased competitive potential with the emerging human brain could have served as the locus of the selection of improved cognitive functions. So, the proposition is that it was not language that drove the evolution of brain morphology, nor was it symbolic, abstract reasoning. The first stage was a relative increase in size of the human brain in proportion to the body. Or, more accurately, the appearance in early humans of a brain designed for a much larger body. How could this have come about in evolutionary terms? Although it may be tempting to claim a role for a superhuman intelligence, there need be no suggestion that any external force undertook these developments. For an explanation we need go no further than Darwin and the fossil record to offer an alternative view.

Discontinuity and Cranial Volume

Referring back to chapter one it will become clear that although there are discontinuities in the fossil evidence regarding human origins such that no firm conclusions can be drawn regarding the last common ancestor, one thing that is certain is that human morphology has changed in a non-linear way over time. Although evidence suggests that the human brain has been increasing in size in a progressive way over the last two million years, such changes are not continuous from *H. habilis* to modern humans. Western *H. erectus* had cranial volumes matching that of modern humans, whilst Neanderthals with cranial volumes of approximately 1300 cc for females and up to 1700 cc for males had larger brains than either *H. erectus* or modern humans. In addition, it is also known from the fossil record that body mass has also change discontinuously over time. *H. erectus* evolved robust forms in the east and more gracile forms in the west, mirroring those of the earliest examples such as West Turkana boy found in Africa. Some developmental strands of *H. erectus* were in fact taller than the mean of modern Europeans, although the gap in average height is decreasing. What this evidence shows is that during early human evolutionary history there were varieties of human ancestors that varied between each other with respect to body size and cranial capacity. It is also known from the fossil record that different species or regional forms overlapped with respect to morphological characteristics. As discussed in chapter one, the Steinheim skull has both Neanderthal and modern characteristics and remains from Caune de l'Arago have features associated with both *H. erectus* and Neanderthals. Now this overlap between the characteristics of distinct human ancestors my be the outcome of a patchwork pattern of evolution, or the result of inter-breeding. One common theory put forward regarding the fate of Neanderthals in Europe is that they inter-bred with a new incoming migration of *H. erectus*, so such supposition is far from fanciful. Now, in line with arguments presented in chapter one, could it be that over time and through many iterations of inter-breeding between different strands of human ancestors with dissimilar brain and body sizes, there arose a faltering transition to an important shift the the brain/body ratio for humankind? Migration from Africa gave rise to multi-regional variation and thus a generation of dissimilar ancestors that could inter-breed at the margins of their populations. Such inter-breeding could give rise to a shift in the brain/body ratio which made possible limited abstract thought by way of the neuronal mechanisms discussed above. If this arose in the way suggested, then these new abilities would become adaptive. However, continuing migration would maintain a degree of geographic isolation which would thus limit the spread of these new characteristics through the early human gene pool. Adaptations elsewhere in response to climatic changes would have ensured that differentiation in form between robust and gracile human ancestors would continue to provide a template for further changes in the brain/body ratio. At this stage of human evolution large climatic changes and variations in sources of food, together with rapid migration and physical diversity linked to continued inter-breeding at the margins of regional formations led to rapid changes in the ratio between the human brain and body such that neuronal natural selection and the process of connective displacement gave rise to a brain that could provide a basis for the development of abstract cognitive abilities. These changes would have taken place in an unpredictable way over the last two million years, culminating in the emergence of modern humans some 200,000 to 100,000 years ago. All that was needed for abstract cognition to emerge was genetic diversity, environmental pressure and natural selection. By chance our ancestors gained in brain slightly larger than needed for the prevailing body size, due to continued diversity and ongoing interbreeding at the margins of populations is became an iterative process and natural selection took care of the rest. A process of discontinuous change from which a potential for enhanced mental abilities emerged.

Now to some readers this may seem a little fanciful as it appears to employ the concept of chance in the equation. There was no direct selective vehicle for abstract mentation, it arose as an unintended consequence of "mismatching" brains and bodies. This mismatching had no adaptive rationale *per se*, it was only when by chance improved cognitive abilities emerged that larger brains in smaller bodies became adaptive. The term for this process of development is of course exaptation, as discussed above. The "final" adaptive trait of abstract cognition did not arise from previous adaptations, but the chance matching of brains and bodies. Further iterations also occurring by chance continued the process. The distinction being made here is crucial to this current analysis. What is being claimed is that the act of inter-breeding between different human ancestors was not of itself adaptive, it did not initially impart a survival advantage to those individuals partaking in cross-group reproduction. Natural selection acts at the level of the individual in terms of setting the context for the existence of differential chances to survive to reproduce. Hence inter-breeding itself is not adaptive and neither is the outcome of larger brains in smaller bodies, it is the improvement in mentation that is adaptive. This means that further acts of inter-breeding between large brained and small bodied hominids would not have been selected for, where it took place it would have arisen by chance; an emergent outcome of a complex system.

The observant reader may have begun to wonder why more than one chance act of inter-breeding is required. Surely once a large brain occupies a small body the natural selection of abstract reasoning would give rise to further evolution of the brain without the need for any further external inputs? Well, I think it is unlikely to be the case that increases in brain size stemmed from the ongoing selection of the very basic level of changes in cognition that occurred at this stage of evolution. There would need to be a threshold of change which would need to have been crossed before any noticeable change in cognitive function could have arisen. Hence it is more likely that first a *capacity* for changes in mentation occurred by way of increased brain size through iterative interbreeding, and only then did some degree of abstract cognition emerge. Best evidence for this comes from the fossil record. Fossil remains do not show a linear progression in morphological change with respect to any characteristic, including increases in brain size. If the first prodigy of the primary interbreeding moment in the genesis of enlarged brains went on to be the true single modern human ancestor, then the fossil record would reveal linear change with regard to brain size. In looking for the most parsimonious explanation, the record can best be described by migration, divergence and subsequent interbreeding.

Notwithstanding the fossil record, there is another reason to suppose that increased brain size in relation to body size did not take place within one direct lineage. Natural selection operates on the basis of increasing fitness at the individual level. There is no reason to suppose that any individual hominid born, through interbreeding with another species, with a relatively enlarged brain would enjoy increased opportunities to survive and reproduce. Even if the first beginnings of abstract thought gave rise to an advantage, it is unlikely to be the case that within early hominids the ability to progress beyond primary consciousness and the relating of current events with past action (see chapter four), would of itself increase chances to reproduce. Primate reproductive strategies are complex, but often depend to a large extent on physical dominance. Although reproduction in these circumstances can occur outwith the control of the dominant male, for example it is known that female chimpanzees will mate covertly with non-dominant males, the balance of evidence suggests that most reproduction occurs as a product of the dominant structure. Of course little is known about the reproductive strategies of *africanus* but it seems unlikely that that they would have departed from primate norms so far as to involve sexual selection around cultural competence. At some unknown point human actions through restructuring the environment did become pivotal in directing evolution, but this could only have taken place once the sharing of abstract ideas became a routine part of social life.

That is, once a recognisable culture had formed. Then, certainly, facility with abstract ideas and language would have been strongly adaptive. Prior to this, however, it is argued that the re-rationg of brain and body was a non-adaptive disjunction in hominid evolution.

So far I have described this process as being dependent on chance, as being emergent. This was merely a convenient way to bracket out any consideration of the mechanism which might underlie such processes until some basic issues had been addressed. Now, however, it needs to be recognised that, as Einstein once remarked, God does not play dice. This means that it cannot be chance in the conventional sense that gave rise to the interbreeding events, there must instead be some underlying mechanism which part informs human evolution that could explain how, systemically, the circumstances from which these proposed moments of interbreeding arose. To understand these processes it is necessary once again to digress into a discussion of some further properties of complex systems and consider strange attractors.

Strange Attractors and Evolution

Dynamic systems, those that change over time, do not evolve at random, but instead follow certain paths. Weather systems, for example, may change rapidly and unpredictably in many cases, but they cannot display absolutely any condition at all from one moment in time to another. For example, in northern Britain in August it cannot be raining at one moment and in the next micro time interval be cloudless and very hot. Of course such differences in the weather can be experienced during the same day but the transition from one state to another will follow on understandable progression of change. The clouds will move away, the rain stop, the sun appear and the temperature slowly rise. The weather system can be said to have moved from state "A" to state "B" by way of an systematic transition. This way of depicting the state of the weather system at a given moment is helpful as it means that at a given moment of time can be described as a single point, state "A" or state "B". For example, it can be said that at time = 0 the weather system is described by state "A", it is raining, and at time + 1 by state "B", it is sunny. State "A" or state "B" can be considered to be single points in the history, or evolution, of the weather system. These single points will be resolutions at specific moments in time of all elements in the system. That is, the rain occurring on that hypothetical August day emerged from a specific configuration at t = 0 of all the elements comprising the weather system (for example, the prevailing winds, local air pressure and position of the jet stream). At $t + 1$ the configuration changed and the system moved along a given trajectory to state "B". Hence, this example shows that it is possible to describe a dynamical system in terms of its status at a given moment in time as being a particular point in its *phase space*. Knowledge about a system can thus be collapsed to a single point, and hence changes in the system can be described as being this single point moving along a given trajectory in phase space such that its status changes over time. This is not to imply that change can follow any trajectory. Particular types of systems follow particular types of trajectory (or produce particular *phase portraits*). The trajectory that a system takes is determined by what is known as an attractor. Hence within complexity theory it is usual to consider the trajectory of change within a system as movement along a specific type of attractor.

Within phase space there are four basic types of attractor. The first depicts a steady state. All points in phase space move towards this attractor and the system comes to rest, hence this attractor is known as a *sink*. This can be depicted by a ball lying at the bottom of a bowl, which will not move unless further energy is applied to the system. Hence a sink is a steady state attractor. The second type of attractor is known as a *source*. This is the inverse of a sink in that all points move away rather than towards the attractor. This can be visualised if you imagine a marble placed on top of a snooker ball. Left alone the marble will not move, but any slight disturbance and the marble will roll down one side. A source is thus a unstable steady state attractor. The third type of attractor is a *saddle*. The best way to imagine movement defined by a saddle is by visualising sitting on a fence with one leg on one side and the other on the opposite side. You would be very stable moving forwards or backwards, but quite unstable moving from side to side. Lines representing forwards and backwards movement would move in towards the saddle and those representing sideways movement would radiate away. Hence where the lines met in the middle would be a steady state. The forth type of attractor is a *limit cycle*, which is not a single point like any of the above attractors, but instead cover a *region* of space. With stable limit cycles adjacent points in phase space move inwards and form a periodic motion, whereas in unstable limit cycles adjacent points move away from each other. Stable limit cycles are thus periodic attractors (they go round and round) and if a number of these, each having a different frequency, are combined a *quasiperiodic attractor* forms. The motion associated with a quasiperiodic attractor can be visualised as loops within loops within loops going around in a circle, describing a donut shape.

From this description of attractors in phase space it is easy to imagine that complex systems over time do one of three things. They stay still unless disrupted and then come to rest at a new steady state, they can follow a predictable periodic motion or, when several periodic attractors combine, they can change by way of a series of integral periodic loops. However, in nature all is not that simple, and there is one further kind of attractor which raises important questions about the ability of science to predict with accuracy transitions in natural systems, such as evolution.

Within many systems the combination of periodic attractors does not give rise to a quasiperiodic attractor, but instead generates a strange attractor (Lorenz 1963). A quasiperiodic attractor arises from the combination of a discrete, finite number of periodic cycles, whereas a strange attractor forms from the formation of a continuum of periodic cycles (more usually in this context referred to as modes or oscillations). In comparison with the predictable movement of a steady-state periodic or quasiperiodic attractor, a strange attractor describes a complex trajectory which is unpredictable. A representation of this can be made by drawing a series of imperfect figures of eight, one each on a single sheet of paper and joined continuously, on an infinite number of sheets of paper. The result would be a trajectory which often returned to a similar point in space (in this exercise each sheet is laid simultaneously next to every other sheet - this can be done in multi-dimensional space) but never fully repeated itself. Remembering that this trajectory, movement on the strange attractor, describes at given moments the status of the system, it can thus be appreciated that the evolution of such a system cannot be predicted with accuracy unless one has complete knowledge of the system. That is, unless the total combined effect of the continuum of modes and the initial starting position of the system was known. Imagine that the point that represents the status of a system which evolves by way of a strange attractor is, for the sake of illustration, a metal ball passing through an asteroid belt with a large large number of asteroids, each of which is affecting both the trajectory of the ball and every other asteroid. Even if the position of the ball at $t = 1$ is known, its position at $t = 2$ could not be predicted unless the summed effect of all the asteroid/ball interactions and the position of the ball at $t = 0$ was also known. That is, knowledge of the evolution of a system defined by a strange attractor is dependent on knowing the initial configuration of the system. This condition is known as sensitive dependence on initial conditions, and it is the most important characteristic of motion on a strange attractor (Ruelle 1993).

So, it appears that change in some types of natural system is not uniform and predictable, but instead discontinuous and unpredictable. In addition, although the system may enter states very similar to any previous state, there will always be differences as the system cannot regain any previous state. Recall the folding of one sheet of paper over another to create a simple multi-dimensional example of a strange attractor. The pen that draws the attractor can only trace a line from one sheet of paper to another continuously, it cannot pass through the paper to a previous position. With respect to a real-world example, one way of understanding this is to appreciate that motion on a strange attractor describes a trajectory through phase space that takes infinite time, consequently the system never repeats itself. Complex, dynamical systems which feature sensitive dependence on initial conditions and change as a motion on a strange attractor are more generally known as complex systems. Complex systems evolve by way of a strange attractor that sometimes gives rise to order and sometimes to chaotic change. In other words, complex systems are thus at times chaotic and at other times ordered. Complex systems can undergo evolution unpredictably because they can become chaotic, but this is not the case in all circumstances and at all times.

As stated above, changes in weather patterns provide a good example of unpredictability in a complex system where change is determined by motion on a strange attractor, and they also show that both order and chaos can occur in such systems. Many natural systems other than weather systems also have these characteristics, even those that are a part of human culture, such as economic or political systems (for example, see Kiel and Elliott 1996). What is being contended here is that the path of human evolution is also best described as motion on a strange attractor. That is, human evolution is a product of change in a dynamic system (the natural world) which is characterised by a continuum of influences (or, in other words, a very large number of determining factors greatly interconnected) and sensitive dependence upon initial conditions.

Having considered some basic characteristics of complex systems this conclusion seems unavoidable. It is beyond dispute that early human evolution took place within a system (nature) with a very large number of interacting determining factors. This means that the path our evolution has taken has been sensitively dependent on initial conditions. Thus, from the basis of complexity theory it has to be conceded that the emergence of our species was an outcome of evolutionary processes which, if they had been configured slightly differently millions of years ago, may never have engendered such an outcome. Indeed the Universe itself would have been very different if the conditions of its emergence had been if slightly different from those which actually took place. As a species humankind is, therefore, travelling through an n-dimensional natural world along the path of a strange attractor such that change, although bounded by species level constraints, is in many ways unpredictable.

So, where does this leave any systematic understanding of human evolution? Does this mean that anything is possible, and if so where does natural selection fit in? Well, this claim is not as radical as it may first seem. The claim that strange attractors are important to understanding human evolution is made purely for the purpose of revealing characteristics of dynamic systems which lead to unpredictable change. Without this understanding, discontinuous change may otherwise be viewed as arising from chance events driven by mechanisms which are beyond any systematic understanding. This is unlikely to be the case in a universe where order is as endemic a feature as chaotic change. Hence, although the most likely explanation for the beginnings of the enlargement of the human brain is some kind of non-adaptive exaptation, and that this temptingly leads to a consideration of the role of chance in human evolution (in the sense of an unsystematic random flux in human history), complexity theory reveals that unpredictability is not unfathomable, but is rather the outcome of specific characteristics of nonlinear dynamic systems. This is because one characteristic of dynamical systems is that the evolution of such systems can be described by movement on a strange attractor. Consequently, such systems can only be completely understood if everything about them, including the complete configuration at $t = 0$ (the exact moment of their appearance), is known. Empirically this is impossible for human evolution as it is an indivisible part of the natural world. Hence, at best, only a small part of our history can be pieced together chronologically in a linear form. The fossil record indicates as much when consideration is given to the mismatch of what are thought to be distinct lineages, the mosaic of different forms found in certain fossil remains. This is not to claim, however, that natural selection is not the central mechanism through which change takes place. The contention is that to grasp more difficult transitions in the human form, an understanding of the nature of complexity is necessary.

Complexity, Natural Selection and the Evolution of Symbolic Reasoning

The preceding discussion has tried to unfold some of the major features of the underlying structure of discontinuous change in natural systems. In this way, where previously appeals to chance have had to be made to explain non-adaptive change, or concepts such as a probable mutation effect contrived, it can be shown that such discontinuous change is an endemic aspect of dynamic system. This is not to claim, however, that anything is possible. Within any natural system there will be system level constraints on what is possible. This can be known theoretically because although, to put it in simple terms, a strange attractor is infinitely long it is nevertheless contained with finite space. And with respect to human evolution, this finite space will be bounded ultimately by the limitations of carbon based life forms, and more specifically (in time periods less than that encompassing the history of humankind) by species level constraints. Depending on the environment, it may be that in tens of millions of years we will become a true aquatic, water-breathing ape, or perhaps something else much more difficult to imagine, but in much smaller time scales what is possible will be constrained by what we are now. Complexity theory thus provides a basis for understanding unpredictable change, but it does not lead to the conclusion that anything is possible at any moment in human history. Big changes which involve substantial morphological shifts can only occur adaptively over long periods of time. But changes in direction, non-linearity, can occur within a dynamic system at any time. Complexity theory allows this to be understood in an abstract way, and the fossil record suggests that this applies to human evolution. The use of this perspective to account for the re-ratioing of hominid brains produces an explanation (migration, divergence, further migration, interbreeding) that both fits the data and has an attractive simplicity. There is no need for sky hooks, hopeful monsters, fantastically contrived mechanisms or the discovery of minute selective advantage to be gained by the addition of a few cells here or there in the human brain. From Deacon's (1997) position on the importance of changes in the brain/body size ratio to the foundation of human symbolic reasoning, what is needed is for a plausible causitive scenario in human evolution to be unfolded. Of course, once it did happen, as a non-adaptive change, then natural selection would lead to the competitive survival of those early humans with this characteristic for whom it proved to be the origin of advantageous behavioural traits. Further changes in brain structure and function would take place adaptively through natural selection as only the initial increase in spare neural capacity was non-adaptive. From that point on in our past, from the neural through to the behavioural level, Darwinian natural selection was the mechanism of further change.

There can be no doubt that Darwinian natural selection is the primary mechanism for evolutionary change in the natural world. However, it has long being recognised by Darwinian scholars from differing perspectives that not all changes are likely to have arisen by direct adaptation. But despite this shared perception in disconnected processes of evolution, there has been little agreement on the nature of such change. Some like Gould have argued for preadaptations without stating how these may have arisen, whereas others like Dennett have preferred to put forward ideas around nested adaptations (where an outcome of previous adaptations can be the unconnected basis for new adaptations). In this chapter it has been argued that with respect to the relative increase in hominid brain size which has taken place during the last 2 million years or so, both adaptation and non-adaptive change will have contributed towards this evolutionary pattern. Human evolution is the outcome of both the emergence of new traits within a non-linear dynamic system and the product of natural selection. Unpredictable, discontinuous events will occur routinely and these will then be subject to natural selection. Often it will be possible to deduce the history of a specific change by way of adaptationist reasoning, but sometimes, as with the case of there being for humankind brains larger than they should be in such a small primate body, this will not be possible and other explanations derived from complexity theory will be necessary. Human life is both adaptive and complex. And a feature of complex dynamic systems is that it is known that sometimes they can be highly unstable and produce rapid change (which may or may not be selected for in evolutionary terms) and at others relatively stable. This, of course, will have profound effects in terms of patterning human life. Consequently, some of the key substantive ramifications for humankind of having cognitive abilities evolved in a complex system will be discussed in chapter three, where the adaptive and rational nature of human cognition will be considered.

3 Cognition and Adaptation

The discussion in chapter two has drawn attention to the way an initial increase in brain capacity in proportion to body size may have arisen. However, notwithstanding this possibility, it remains the case that the emergence of specific enhanced cognitive abilities occurred by way of natural selection. As was discussed previously, even the development of neural inputs and outputs occurs competitively in a selective environment. Hence, although the volume of certain areas of the brain may have increased relative to the normative demands of a hominid body non-adaptively, the new functions which subsequently arose would have done so by way of natural selection: that is, through competition with other possible novel inputs and outputs. From what is already known about neural developmental processes from findings in evolutionary neuroscience by such as those of Edelman and Deacon, once spare neural capacity emerged competition would have set the context for any restructuring of hominid mental life that subsequently took place. In circumstances defined by competition in biological systems, those traits or functions that succeeded would have been those that best enhanced either survival and reproduction. In these cases, no other explanation is needed, this is the standard Darwinian position on natural selection, but, of course, more is needed to establish this argument than a mere assertion. If it is the case that the characteristics of human cognition are adaptive, then it should be possible to outline the process through which the cognitive life of modern humans arose. So why did symbolic reasoning emerge from the expansion of cranial capacity outlined in chapter two instead of, say, enhanced audio abilities as with dolphins and other cetaceans? Well, it must have something to do with the context of early hominid life. Something that led to an advantage being gained by those early ancestors that first displayed an ability to think abstractly.

In looking for a candidate for the role of founder of the emergence of abstract thought, there are a number of candidates. Throughout much of the literature it is held that early human creativity was primarily divergent from the behaviour of other primates in terms of either language or the manufacture and use of tools, though social life too has been suggested as the starting point for cognitive evolution. This latter approach will be returned to below, but first a possible relationship between language and tool-making will be unfolded.

Being able to engage in complex communication or manipulate the environment through making and using tools are both categories of action that would impart advantage in terms of survival and reproduction, and both require an ability to categorise information and to think symbolically. It is fairly easy to think of reasons why language or tool use impart an advantage in terms of survival and reproduction. Being able to communicate complex information about the environment would mean that knowledge of how best to exploit a habitat could be shared between members of a group and subsequently passed on to offspring. This would clearly give an advantage to those either possessing or best able to exploit this ability. Similarly, tool making and usage would mean that additional sources of food would be made available as previously inaccessible supplies could be acquired (say, through digging) or more effective means of defence against predators achieved. However, why are both of these attributes thought to be based upon abstract thought? Why is it being suggested that these two seemingly different abilities are somehow linked.

It is, perhaps, relatively easy to understanding the abstract basis of language. After all, language is the gestured, written or spoken representation of reasoning about the external world and our ourselves. This is not to suggest that it is simply this, any complete evaluation must also account for the fact that a significant proportion of human cognition is grounded in language, so language is not just a tool. Nonetheless, this simple definition draws attention to the symbolic status of language. Having reasoned about the world either consciously or otherwise, when we communicate the products of our contemplation it is necessary to employ known and shared representations of these ideas from a given language. Ideas and language are not one, as anyone who has struggled with ideas beyond their ability to express them in a written form may testify. Some may take issue with this rather brief way I have defined language, but my purpose here, at this stage, is to establish only that language is a means of representing the external world symbolically, rather than to claim that language is an unproblematic part of the social world.

So, language use is based upon abstraction and symbolisation, but can the same be argued for tool making and use? Although it may seem that language and tool use are different categories of action quite separate in substance, they both have in common the need to categorise objects in an abstract manner. For example, a screwdriver or a hammer are not merely physical objects that are named as "tools" associated with a single function, but are instead implements with a particular design that can be utilised for a variety of functions. A hammer is primarily used to hit something with, usually a nail or tack, but it can also be used as a weapon, as a device with which to open a can or a jar, to crack a nut or to break something, such as a window (and I am sure you can think of many other uses). The fact that the tasks in the second category are not best undertaken with a hammer, as some other tool would be more appropriate, does not matter. Even if these are inefficient ways to complete the task set, they can nevertheless be undertaken with a hammer if that was all that was available. Similarly, although a screwdriver has a primary intended use as a means to remove screws, it too can be used as a weapon, to open a can, to crack (or more accurately, to lever) open a nut and to break something. Nevertheless, when shown a hammer and asked to classify it in terms of its function you would do this differently than with respect to a screwdriver. However, there would be overlap between the two at some levels of classification (they are both tools with which mechanical tasks are achieved) even though at the base level the hammer would be a "hitting" tool and the screwdriver a "turning" tool. Now these various categories of use, from the base level through to more generic classes are not naturally occurring, but have instead being created cognitively in relation to both the behavioural tasks it is necessary sometimes to complete, and the tools manufactured to achieve that function. In this way the hammer or the screwdriver become to be known as not merely as objects constructed of metal and wood, but also as representations of particular functions. If asked to do so, the reader would be able to construct an elaborate framework of interconnections of function (and thus designations) for the hammer and the screwdriver, and for other tools, starting from the simple description of various uses given above and progressing to include an assessment of suitability of particular functions. This would be an exercise in symbolic reasoning in that the tool item would become less a physical object than a graded abstraction of possible functions.

What is being argued here is that symbolic reasoning comes into being at the point at which the identification of an object transcends mere naming and encompasses abstract generalisation. The hammer and the screwdriver are assigned multi-category identities related to particular functions. Deacon (1997) has discussed this process of moving from the naming of objects to abstract categorisation in terms of a transition from iconic relationships, through indexical relationship to to symbolic relationships. In Deacon's analysis iconic relationships refer to the simple recognition of an object, that is, knowing what the item or event is; such as, "this is a hammer". Indexical relationships are those which are formed from relationships between icons. For example, the perception of a nut triggers the thought of a hammer with which to crack open the nut (of course we would actually use nutcrackers, but they did not exist in the times of our hominid ancestors). This is a higher order level of organising information about the external world. Through learning about associations between icons, indexical relationships are formed. Symbolic relationships, Deacon argues, arise when words are used to denote associations between indexical relationships. So, to provide an example of this a new tool will be depicted for the foraging activities of a our hominid ancestor.

The hypothetical hominid ancestor already knows about "hammers" and nuts. Later, through developing associations there has arisen a further pattern of cognition and behaviour such that when an item of fruit is located high in a tree beyond reach, a stick is found with which to dislodge the fruit. So there would then be two indexical relationships which have developed through association. These would be, "hammer-nut" and "fruit-stick". Now suppose that a new task presented itself to our ancestor, perhaps a root trapped out of reach between rocks. Our ancestor could think "fruit-stick" (a root perhaps being like a fruit in this case) and thus draw on an indexical relationship. Indeed it is probable that this stretching of indexical relationships did occur at some time in human history. Now at some point, when increased brain capacity provided the potential for such development, the new task will have been reasoned as "hammer-nut + fruit-stick = tool". That is, the notion of a generic class "tool" which combines indexical relationships will have emerged. With this insight the hominid would then be more disposed towards investigating the environment for a tool that works to help solve a new problem. The idea of a "tool" is thus a symbol for task solving indices. Now, this description of the emergence of symbolic reasoning does not depend on there being a word "tool" which is spoken or otherwise communicated. All that is necessary is that the cognition of an association higher than an indexical relationship occurs.

What is being argued here is that although I agree with Deacon's use of nested hierarchies of association as being a possible basis for the formation of symbolic reasoning, I maintain that language is not a necessary condition for this to emerge. Although I have no systematic evidence at hand to support this contention, it nevertheless seems from informal observation that a human ability to reason associations outside formal language may be common. A case-study cited by Lecours and Joanette (1980) provides evidence for the contention that not all cognition is dependent on language. They cite the case of

"Brother John", a 50 year old man who edited letters for a religious order. Brother John suffered epileptic seizures for 25 years. He experienced short attacks lasting one to five minutes five times each day, and long attacks lasting between one and 11 hours once a month. Theses seizures affected the left side of the brain and selectively restricted his language processing ability such that he experienced periods of aphasia. His seizures gave rise to a complex pattern of effects changing over the duration of the attack from global aphasia to an inability to comprehend, through a period where he had an inability to comprehend to a disorder of repetition and then amnesia. However, even in the most extreme stages of a seizure Brother John was consciously aware of the effects of his disability and was able to continue to function in complex settings. When once travelling to Switzerland he experienced an attack, but despite his aphasia he was able to collect is luggage, find a first hotel that proved to be unhelpful, find a second, gesture to his passport for registration information, find the hotel restaurant and order a meal by indicating a choice (through guesswork) on the menu. He then returned to his hotel room for the night. Despite his inability to use or perceive language, he was thus able to cope with complex social events in an unfamiliar hotel setting. It is reported that he retained coherent thought around music, voices, faces, locations and objects. Clearly, the absence of language does not imply the absence of complex patterns of cognition typically found with non-aphasic subjects. We can reason by other means than by way of language based concepts. Whilst engaging in research activities I have many times had insights into underlying patterns that I have struggled only partly successfully to write down and pass on to others. Sometimes language seems as much a barrier to creative thought as an assistance!

It would appear from the above discussion that the evolution of tool use may have been the initial starting point for the development of symbolic reasoning in humankind. It may have been only later that language emerged, as symbolic categories such as "tool" began to be verbalised to pass on abstract information. There is, though, an alternative perspective. It may be that tool-making and language co-evolved as the foundation of human reasoning. This issue is of more than passing interest as any understanding the nature of human cognition must, at least in part, include an understanding of the way it unfolded in our evolutionary past. The origins of symbolic reasoning will to some extent determine its scope and limitations. In other words, the basis from which symbolic reasoning formed will, at least in part, determine its nature. Although it may not be possible for the actual chronology of these events to be uncovered (not least because of the emergent character of outcomes that occur within complex systems, as outline above), archeological and fossil evidence offer important insights into the timing of changes to areas of the brain associated with language, manual dexterity and other related cognitive functions.

Tools, Language and the Emergence of Symbolic Reasoning

Although some anthropologists have argued that it is unlikely that human ancestors as recent as Neanderthals were able to speak (Lieberman and Crelin 1971), fossil evidence of the development of certain areas of the brain in fact suggest that a spoken language may have appeared as long as two million years ago. The evidence for this stems from research carried out on the enlargement of certain areas of the brain known to be involved in aspects of speech. These are Broca's and Wernicke's areas. Broca's area is located in the dominant hemisphere of the brain (which is usually the left hemisphere) and is multi-functional. Its functions are concerned with the storage and automation of sequential activities which enable an animal to learn, store and perform complex motor task as a single act, including the voluntary control of verbalisation (Lieberman 1994). Wernicke's area is associated with the storage of words.

It is studies of dysfunctions in either Broca's or Wernicke's areas that have led to the uncovering of the role that each of these areas serves in the use of language. Damage to Broca's area results in a wide range of aphasic (language-use related) dysfunctions. When pathways to the prefrontal cortex are damaged, control of the vocal tract and larynx is disrupted, and the comprehension of syntax can be adversely affected. Such language deficiency involves the loss of the use of grammatical variation, such as being unable to employ or understand the use of articles, conjunctions and prepositions (Lieberman 1994). Further studies of aphasia show that damage to Wernicke's area leads to difficulties in the selection of words. Those suffering from Wernicke's aphasia use words that are out of context or meaningless. Consequently, from this research, it is known that each of these areas, in conjunction with the prefrontal cortex, are closely involved in the production of speech. Hence many researchers have concluded that studies of the growth of these areas over time in human ancestors may lead to insights into the timing and process of the evolution of language.

Research seeking to reveal the structure of hominid brains frequently makes use of endocasts (where an imprint of the inside of a skull is used to assess the degree of development of certain regions of the brain). By this means it has been established that a bulge over Broca's area, which is known as Broca's cap, has been found to be a feature of the brain of *A. africanus* (Schepers 1946, 1950; Tobias 1983). This is not, however, a feature of the contemporary ape brain. With respect to Wernicke's area, there is no related morphological projection in either ape brains or *A. africanus* , but there is one present in *H. habilis* (Tobias 1994). In addition, Falk (1983) has revealed that the frontal lobes of modern human differ significantly between contemporary apes and *A. africanus*, but are very similar to *H. habilis*. This research has led Tobias (1981, 1983) to suggest that *H. habilis* had the necessary neurological basis for the presence of speech. Hence, it was argued that spoken language appeared some two million years ago, much earlier than proposed by those many researchers who, based on assessments of the absence of developments in the vocal tract and larynx until relatively recently, claim a history of perhaps only 40,000 years.

Tobias (1994) argues that although morphological developments to the vocal tract and larynx clearly contribute to the phonetic forms of contemporary speech, they are not, in their current structure, a necessary condition for speech. He maintains that a relatively small number of speech sounds would not of itself exclude vocalisation from being classified as a spoken language. Indeed, this may be the case as the linguistic status or otherwise of vocalisations would depend on the presence or absence of symbolisation and grammatical structure rather than the number of sounds being uttered. Tobias (1994) notes that Lieberman (1988) endorses the view that *H. Habilis* remains do show the early signs of the development of a contemporary human vocal tract, so hence it is becoming widely accepted that *H.habilis* could well have been the first speaking primate.

This may indeed have been the case, but what does this research have to contribute to establishing the nature of the developments antecedent to the emergence of symbolic reasoning and a spoken language? Well, these findings show that the development of Broca's area began, in evolutionary terms, prior to those of Wernicke's area and the prefrontal cortex. It is generally believed that *A. africanus* first appeared some two to three million years ago, compared with from 1.5 to two million years ago for *H. habilis*. Now, given that although Broca's area is associated with speech it is accepted that it is unlikely that *A. africanus* was a speaking primate (given the lack of appropriate developments in the frontal cortex or Wernicke's area) it must therefore be the case that Broca's area originally evolved to fulfil another function. In fact is has been known for some time that in addition to fulfilling functions with regard to speech, Broca's area is also involved in motor function. Kimura (1979) and Stuss and Benson (1986) have shown that in addition to language functions, Broca's area is also involved in accurate motion of the dominant hand. And Lieberman (1994) notes that as many animals other than humankind show hand or paw preference, the origin of Broca's area may be other than via speech. Hence, as Lieberman (1994) maintains, brain mechanisms that moderate speech appear to have antecedents in hand or paw movements. And, further to this, Kimura (1979) argues that Broca's area may have evolved initially in relation to precise actions by the dominant hand.

This may be so, but it is a long way from precise hand movements and the early development of Broca's area to symbolic reasoning and modern human speech. That is unless the analysis presented above, which argued for a beginning of symbolic reasoning by way of tool manufacture and use, is recalled. If, as was argued, tool use and manufacture was the key antecedent to the development of symbolic reasoning, then it would be expected that those areas must closely associated with manual dexterity would appear prior to those solely linked (as far as is known at present) to language functions. Given that it is known that Broca's area did appear prior to Wernicke's area and the expansion of the prefrontal cortex, then this hypothesis may be somewhat more formally established. Further support is provided by Wynn (1994) who noted that as preference for one hand over another (handedness) is linked to morphological asymmetries of the brain, tool behaviour (precise manual dexterity) may have selected for distinct adaptations in neural structures. A position supported by Frost (1980), for whom handedness and asymmetries in brain structure were selected for by tool manufacture and use (cited in Wynn 1994).

Assuming that this is the case, what is the link from this to language and symbolic reasoning? Well, it would seem from the evidence cited that a certain sequence of development from a pre-symbolic consciousness can be discerned. Prior to *A. africanus* there is no evidence from the fossil record that hominid brains differed in any notable way from other early primates and contemporary apes. At around two to three million years ago *africanus* appeared and with this species there appears to have been the beginnings of development in Broca's area. However, given that there were no related developments in the prefrontal cortex or Wernicke's area it is generally assumed that *africanus* did not speak. This suggests that the enlargement of Broca's area arose from some other selective pressure, and the association of this region of the brain with precise manual coordination suggests that tool use may have been the adaptive force structuring change. Tobias (1994) notes that traces of stone tools found at Hadar in Ethiopia by Corvinas have been dated between 2.7 and 2.4 million years ago (Corvinas 1976). This finding demonstrates the existence of stone tools prior to the arrival of *H. habilis*. So, the first evidence of brain evolution taking place in the direction of modern human forms appears to be correlated not with language, but with tool use. Perhaps initially changes were related only to the use of tools, a behavioural trait common amongst other primates such as chimpanzees. But at some stage tool use evolved to tool manufacture, an activity requiring some degree of symbolic reasoning as outlined above. Of course in the early stages of the transition into a tool-making species, progress would have been imperceptible, but what would have distinguished such use from that of other primates would have been *change*. That is, *africanus* would have begun to modify tools to achieve new functions to solve novel problems. This is an aspect of tool use which has not been observed with other primate tool users, where despite the presence of a diversity of tool use, especially amongst chimpanzees, tools are not modified to meet new needs (though it remains a possibility that such changes are occurring so slowly over time, in a true Darwinian fashion, that they have not been observed) (see Wynn 1994). Once this process began with *africanus* it would most likely become strongly adaptive, and thus continued within both the *Australopithecus* and *Homo* lines. The best tool makers gained the best survival and reproduction rates and natural selection gave rise to further adaptation in neural structures. It is known that Broca's area functions in connection with the prefrontal cortex, the site of creative mentation, hence processes of adaptation possibly first led to greater integration between Broca's area and an emerging cortex. Clearly proficiency in the manufacture and use of tools with which to improve the exploitation of food sources would require not only high levels of manual dexterity but also, as outlined above, some ability to think abstractly. In time, with the emergence of *H. habilis* (whose cranial capacity was some 40% greater than *africanus*), adaptations in neural structures may have led to a modest ability to communicate abstract thoughts through a spoken language which, though phonetically limited due to the lack of development to the vocal tract and larynx, would have imparted a further survival advantage. Once these building blocks of language and symbolic reasoning were in place, natural selection would have ensured a continuous process of development.

Although there is evidence to support this sequence of continuous change it should not be forgotten that there remains, from this perspective, a need to explain why these changes took place with regard to the hominids and not other primates. In this regard the discussion in chapter two regarding the re-ratioing of the relationship between brain and body size should not be forgotten. As Tobias (1994) noted, the period of from two to three million years ago was a time of great climactic change in the hominid environment. With the cooling and aridification of Africa and the development of woodland and growth in savanna area occurring together with dramatic changes in African mammalian fauna. In consequence of such changes there existed several different types of hominid around this time; *A. africanus* (two to three million years ago), *A. robustus* (one to two million years ago), *A. boisei* (one to two million years ago), *H. habilis* (similar time before the present) and *H. erectus* (appearing around 1.7 million years ago. Hence this appears to have been a time of dramatic variation in hominid evolution, with different types coexisting in the same habitat. Taking this together with evidence of migratory behaviour amongst early human ancestors, and including and consideration of the resultant potential for inbreeding between hominids with different morphology, the argument returns to the case for the relative enlargement of the brain discussed in chapter two.

Although fossil remains of both large and small bodied *H. habilis* have been found (Stringer and Gamble 1993) there is in general a lack of fossil evidence to support this contention with respect to very early events in this period (compared with more recent examples of Homo, as discussed in chapter one). Nevertheless, given what is known about environmental changes in the late Pliocene and the diversity of Hominid types, it is perhaps not unreasonable to suppose that the process of migration, adaptation, re-migration and interbreeding outlined in chapter two actually began quite distantly in the Hominid past. Consequently, although it is possible to sequence stages of the development of symbolic reasoning, this must be seen as occurring within the context of nonlinear exapted change in the amount of brain volume available for neurological restructuring and re-functioning. If not, then another explanation must be sought for the large-scale move from non-developmental tool use still common amongst some current primates to the creative, problem solving tool manufacture of Hominids. Any such explanation could only be based on environmental considerations, and in that regard it seems that the explanation is already at hand! If, within a dissimilar group of crude tool users dwelling in a rapidly changing environment, you mix different size bodies with different size brains, add a large dose of natural selection and then wait long enough, something interesting and new will surely happen! On this planet, this is perhaps what emerged. It may never have happened, but this time around it did!

So where does this discussion take us with respect to understanding not only some of the processes of human evolution but the basic nature of human mental life as well? Obviously knowledge about the beginnings of humankind are important in its own right. Human beings like to solve problems even if solving a particular problem does not have an immediate practical purpose. But knowledge about the very starting point of our particular kind of intelligence can provide insights into other aspects of human cognition. If human symbolic reasoning evolved in a particular set of circumstances to solve particular types of problem then, from an adaptationist perspective, these founding conditions should be located in the way modern humans think. What this means is that our ability to reason will not be without boundaries, but will instead be structured in important ways by our evolutionary past. Perhaps the reason why we are inveterate problem solvers and like to unravel puzzles and riddles is because it all started with the emergence of creative tool use and tool making? Although it is common to refer to humankind as the speaking ape, perhaps the problem-solving primate is our true first ancestor?

Adaptation and the Nature of Human Cognition

Beneath such a simple statement lies an important conclusion about the nature of human cognition. By suggesting that a fascination with puzzles and riddles may be linked to the first rudimentary experiments with tool making by our ancestors, it is being implied that the beginnings of abstract reasoning may determine one important component of modern human cognition. This is to argue that human cognition is adaptive; the product of natural selection. Instead of being in possession of a rational computer capable of any kind of abstract problem solving, we have instead a mind which has evolved to unravel particular types of problems. Namely, initially those related to issues of survival or reproduction. One consequence of this aspect of human cognition would be that the ability to solve a problem would be less related to its difficultly than its relationship to the circumstances of life from which abstract reasoning stemmed. Human beings, for example, are much better at understanding visual data than numerical data. Data showing the relationship between annual expenditure on pensions and age distribution in a population is more easily discerned with pie charts and graphs than pages full of raw correlations. The reason that a picture does indeed convey more information than a thousand numbers (or words) is that humankind evolved in a visual and not a numerical world. Even the seemingly most cognitively simple behaviours, such as playing a game of squash, are in fact the outcome of extremely complex judgments of the real-time movement of objects in three dimensional space. We, and other mammals, find such determinations simple, merely a reflex behaviour with an intended outcome - there is the ball, I want it over here, so I move and hit it just so. The ease with which we find such high paced physical activity in three dimensional space is deceptive. Currently it is not possible to build a computer that could calculate fast enough to play a human opponent and equal the variety shots, tactics and strategies used in only an average level game. Modern humans may not be able to complete arithmetical problems as quickly as a computer can, but with respect to tasks related to the environment within which humankind evolved natural selection still has the best designs.

This is not to claim that humankind will always out perform computers on all tasks at which we currently do best. In time it may be possible that computers will surpass us at processing visual and spatial problems. The purpose of the example was to demonstrate that what limits human cognition is not complexity, but the nature of the problem. Remembering a list of 24 dictated numbers and being able to recite these instantly in reverse order is computationally simple, but extremely difficult for the average person to complete successfully. Flying a modern fast jet inverted at 500 miles a hour through mountainous terrain whilst simultaneously deploying weapons systems is only achieved by way of the resolution of complex visual, spatial and audio data, but hundreds of trained pilots do this routinely every day. So, human cognition is not framed by levels of complexity, but by the nature of the problem encountered. It is a matter of quality not quantity.

From studies in evolutionary psychology analyses of the role that natural selection has played in forming human cognition are becoming more widespread. Early work by Wason (1972) on the way people solved logical problems provided the first systematic studies of this kind. Wason was interested in uncovering fundamental principles that underlie deductive reasoning. To test the way logical abstract problems are solved he devised an experiment in which subjects were tested on their ability to detect violations of the conditional rule *If P then Q*.

Each subject was given a number of cards with a letter on one side and a number on the other. They were then asked to select which cards they would have to turn over to determine if the rule "if a card has a vowel on one side then it has a a an even number on the other" was true or false. In effect, they were being asked to determine whether or not the experimenter was, by way of the rule, telling the truth. The correct response is to only choose cards with a vowel (P) and without an even number (not-Q), but the majority of subjects selected cards with a vowel and with an even number (P and Q). This response is incorrect because the rule says nothing about consonants. It does not matter if an even number is matched with a consonant, they do not count in testing the rule. Subjects realised this in not selecting cards showing consonants (not-P), but failed to do so with respect to cards showing even numbers. The conclusion from Wason's research is that people in general have difficulty with deductive reasoning involving test of validity of the rule; If P then not Q.

In many ways this is an unsatisfactory conclusion in terms of the analysis being presented in this current book. It has been argued above that rather than language being the starting point of abstract reasoning, it was instead tool making and tool use through the emergence as symbolic reasoning around ancestral problem solving by *africanus*. However, an implication of this natural history of cognition is that it may be fair to assume that an intelligence that emerged by way of natural selection would operate best in circumstances that were historically meaningful.

The Logic of Social Exchange

The view that the nature of human cognition will reflect historical, evolutionary concerns is not new. From the early work of Wason other researchers have devised experiments on the quality of human deductive reasoning. Plotkin (1994) cited findings from further research on P and not-Q test of validity structured on the basis of meaningful tasks facing nightclub security guards. In the test subjects were asked to select which cards they would need to select to determine whether a rule which prohibits drinking alcohol under the age of twenty years was being broken. the cards they were presented with were drinking beer (P), drinking coke (not-P), more than twenty years of age (Q) or less than twenty years of age (not-Q). Unlike with the Wason test where few gave the correct answer (P and not-Q), 75% gained the right answer in this research. Although the reason for P and not-Q being the correct answer in the Wason test, it can be readily appreciated this is the correct answer in this latter case as security guards concerned with under-age drinking would not be interested in the age of coke drinkers (not-P) or the drinking preferences of those aged over twenty years. Thus people are good at P and not-Q test of validity when the subject matter has meaningful content. As simple as these tests are, they do provide some evidence in support of the contention that human reasoning is adaptive.

Taken together these two experiments are helpful in building up evidence for the existence of an adaptive component to human reasoning, but the evidence is not conclusive as in the case of the nightclub security guards the scenario depicted is hardly one within which modern human intelligence could have emerged through natural selection. If evidence is to be presented then it needs to be constructed in terms of situations logically consistent with satisfactory depictions of environments likely to have been encountered by our ancestors. This requirement was recognised by Leda Cosmides, an evolutionary psychologist who carried out a programme of studies in the 1980s on what she termed the logic of social exchange. Cosmides (1989) had noted that the study of human reasoning up until that time had been dominated by research on content-dependent cognitive processes. She argued that early research had been based on the assumption that human beings reasoned logically from some content independent inferential process. However, over time it had become apparent that people do not reason from the basis of an abstract formal logic, but instead are dependent on the context of the problem. People reason according to the context of the subject, as shown above when results from abstract P and not-Q test of validity are compared with those based on a meaningful context.

Cosmides's position was based on the view that people are not particularly good at problems unrelated to particular context encountered during the process of evolution. Cosmides (1989) argued that the human mind did not emerge with a predisposition to solve arbitrary tasks, but instead arose with a capability to solve problems encountered within primal environments. From this basis Cosmides proposed that people would be specifically good at solving problems related to rules of social exchange. Social exchange being a term used to describe the exchange of goods or labour in a social context. Being an essential part of human social life, Cosmides argued that it should be possible to demonstrate that people are particularly competent at such forms of problems. Or more specifically, people would have evolved to be skilled at detecting when rules of social exchange were violated. And the situations chosen to represent this general facility were concerned with the evaluation of cost-benefit transactions. That is, an assessment of whether if someone gains a benefit they pay the associated price.

To test the hypothesis that people would have evolved with a specific facility at such tasks, Cosmides devised a version of the Wason selection test. She devised rules of the general form "If you take the benefit then you pay the price", but which would nevertheless be unfamiliar to subjects in terms of content. The actual terms chosen were somewhat obscure so that the results of the experiment would avoid being interpreted as arising from the current familiarity of the subjects with the subject area (as may be claimed with respect to the research cited that was based upon detecting underage drinking). The research problem in Cosmides's work is set in a hypothetical situation related to the exchange of goods in in a primal society. In Dean (1997) a simplified account of this research was presented, and this will be drawn on here to illustrate to the reader the broad findings of this research. Those readers who require further detail of this innovative research are recommended to read the original findings in Cosmides (1989).

In Dean (1997) the problem presented to subjects in Cosmides's work was reframed to relate to the law "If you want a hut, then you must fell a tree". As with other versions of the Wason selection test subjects were asked to determine by selecting relevant cards whether or not the law was being upheld. In this simplified example they would thus be presented with four cards; has a hut (P), does not have a hut (not-P), felled a tree (Q), did not fell a tree (not-Q). As is usual with this test, each card will have on the reverse side whether they have felled a tree for cards about huts, and whether they had a hut for those cards referring to felling trees. As the reader will have ascertained, the correct response would be P and not-Q, because as the leader of this tribe you are only interested in establishing if someone had a hut they would have felled a tree. Consequently you check the card "P" to see if it was matched with felling a tree, and card not-Q to see if felling a tree was matched with having a hut. As tribal leader you would not be interested in those who did not have a hut (not-P) and those who felled a tree (Q). Thus these results are the same as with respect to the selection test on underage drinking. Cosmides, though, took the research a stage further and reversed the way the law could be falsified. Instead of checking a law of the form given in this simplified case "If you want a hut then you must fell a tree", the subjects were presented with a switched law of the form "If you fell a tree then you will be given a hut". The logical falsifiers of this rule are the same as with the non-switched version of the law; that is, P and not-Q. You would check to ensure that those who felled a tree (P) had a hut, and those who did not have a hut (not-Q) had not felled a tree. The results that Cosmides obtained from a switched test of this type were, however, different from that expected. The majority of respondents selected "did not fell a tree (not-P) and did have a hut (Q). That is, they were checking to see if those who had not felled a tree in fact did have a hut. In other words, as Cosmides explains, they were looking for "cheaters", those who received the reward but did not pay the price. She argues that the reason for this is adaptive in that in resolving P and not-Q test of validity there has been selected as a component of human cognition a "Darwinian algorithm" for "looking for cheaters". In general, such Darwinian algorithms form a base-line structure for human deductive reasoning which is the product of natural selection. In this sense it can be argued that some important part of human cognition is in the form of an adaptive rationality in that we solve problems and come to logical conclusions often not on the basis of a formal logic derived of abstract science, but instead on the basis of a reasoning process which in many respects mirrors the concerns of our more distant evolutionary past. In chapter two there was some discussion of the way that natural selection operates at the neural level in both the formation of neural networks which underpin perception and consciousness, as described by Edelman, and in the competition for neural tissue that may take place between perceptual functions, as described in Deacon's work. Thus, as has previously been established, natural selection operates at the neural level during the formation of physical networks, and now Cosmides's work shows how this may be reflected in the structure of human cognition.

Edelman's research (1992) has illustrated some principles of how the selection of neural networks may be affected by external, environmental events. He argued that when first encountering in external world a number of different neural pathways will be present that could serve to elicit a particular response. Early on in developmental processes each of these will have an equal chance of being selected as the most appropriate vector for the chosen action or cognition, but as each is triggered over time one will eventually be established as the most appropriate for the target function. This pathway will be triggered more often than those less suited, and in consequence the selected pathway will endure and be strengthened whilst others less suited will degenerate relatively. An example commonly given refers to the seemingly random movements of a new born child which appear initially undirected, but eventually lead to success in clutching a bottle, touching a face or achieving some other intentional reaction. The initial random movements will stem from the excitation of many competing neural pathways, these will then eventually be reduced to those which result in the best execution of, in this case, the target behaviour. Recalling that neural pathways do not function individually, but instead form neural networks interconnected with other neural networks, it is possible to envision a process of increasing complexity in stages of operation such that at a higher-order level neural networks involved in cognitive processes were selected for through experiencing the social environment.

If this is so, and the evidence presented supports the concept of an adaptive rationality being a component of human cognition, then it is reasonable to speculate on whether moral judgment have also arisen by way of natural selection. Cosmides (1989) has speculated on this possibility by considering whether or not there may be a deontic logic as a component of human cognition. Manktelow and Over (1987) raised the possibility of the existence of a "moral logic", but Cosmides (1989) concludes that such a theory would not adequately explain her findings. Whilst acknowledging that a "look for cheaters" strategy does in some way include rules relating to obligations and entitlements, she argues that a rule which incorporates entitlements and obligations but does not have a cost-benefit framework would not give rise to the responses noted in her research. As noted in Dean (1997), this is a satisfactory conclusion as to argue otherwise is to engage in a reductionist process whereby one cognitive process can only be understood by way of an other operating at a lower level. However, this does not mean that a deontic logic is not a component of human cognition.

The possibility that value, the quality of experience, may be linked biologically to higher-order symbolic mentation is expressed in Edelman's research. Edelman (1992) has argued that the reentrant linkages between different neural networks are extended between different brain regions such that higher-order consciousness is linked by way of neurophysiological structures to evolutionarily primitive areas of the brain associated with eating, drinking, sexual behaviour and emotive arousal, the brain stem and the limbic system. For Edelman, the evolution of the cortical system took place within the context of adaptive learning behaviour directed towards satisfying physiological needs and values mediated by the limbic-brain stem system. Thus the categorisation of the external world seen as a function of the cortex was linked to the value function of this neural system. The consequence of this co-evolution, argues Edelman, is that symbolic categorisation occurs within the context of a physiological value system. Hence adaptive changes in behaviour, underpinned by cognitive events, are structured in relation to adaptive values. Thus values associated with hunger, sex and emotive arousal are linked physiologically with higher-order cognitive functions.

This is not to argue, however, that everything we do is structured in relation to food, sex and other physical and emotional pleasures, at least not in the sense of any simple one-to-one relationship. However the existence such linkages is clearly supported from a theoretical, adaptationist perspective, and this suggests that even higher-order cognitive functions may be grounded to some unknown degree in very primitive brain functions. One boundary of human consciousness may be the nature of ancestral instincts.

If, as appears to be the case, there exists within human consciousness a component related to the gratification of hunger and sex, and emotive arousal, then it seems likely that human adaptive reasoning does comprise an element of deontic logic. For example, it seems reasonable to suppose that children trigger changes in levels of emotive arousal, and that emotive responses to physical and emotional well-being of children are very primitive. If this is so, then the base region of such responses (where they originated in evolutionary terms) would be the limbic-brain stem region. This, as we know from Edelman's work, became linked through co-evolution with higher-order cognitive functions, hence it would be expected that the adaptive rationality that arose from these processes would have formed, in part, around issues related to emotional arousal associated with child care. Recalling that humankind is a collective, social species then this child-centred component of adaptive rationality would be given expression through a social logic not dissimilar in type to that governing social exchange. An untested proposal for a P and not-Q test of validity which may examine the existence or otherwise of a deontic logic in human reasoning was presented in Dean (1997). In testing for a deontic logic it can be hypothesised that instead of a "look for cheaters" strategy, the major focus would be on a "look for disadvantage" strategy. By using a Wason selection test to see if the rule "If a child sits by the fire then they must have chopped some wood" would, by way of looking for disadvantage, be not-P and Q (the reverse of a look for cheaters strategy). Similarly, in a switched the switched version "If a child chops some wood then they can sit by the fire" would give rise to a P and not-Q response. The adaptive, deontic logic would be directed towards ensuring that no child would be unjustly excluded from the fire. A logic of this type would be adaptive in that for some period of a child's life they would need to be protected from being disadvantaged by adult competition.

So far the current analysis lends support to a multi-dimensionality in human cognition. It has been argued that the starting point was tool-making, that led in turn to language, but what has not been acknowledge so far is the possible role that human social life may have played in the evolution of these or other human cognitive traits. The fact that humankind is a social primate cannot be overlooked. Notwithstanding a belief in the genesis of language by way of tool-making, the demands of hominid social life must have influenced strongly the form that language took. As it has been argued that there was co-evolution between language and the brain, so too must it be considered that there was co-evolution between language and the character of hominid social life. Symbolic reasoning ability led to the acquisition of language within the context of a hominid social world. This must have influenced both the way language was used and its relationship to other aspects of an complex emerging mental life. It is necessary, therefore, to consider to social basis of the evolution of human cognition.

Social Life and Machiavellian Intelligence

In addition to the focus on language and tool-making, there is perhaps one other important component in the genesis of modern human cognition. Robin Dunbar has argued that early human social life provided the circumstances for changes in patterns of interaction around grooming and other key aspects of early hominid social life that led, interactively, to improved cognitive abilities and the emergence of language. The roots of this approach can be found in developments in evolutionary psychology in the 1970s. The key paper from this area focused on what was termed the social function of intellect (Humphrey 1976). It was argued that as primate social life is associated with complex relationships around cooperation and opposition, an ability to anticipate the actions of others would impart a survival advantage. That is, an ability to predetermine the behaviour of others in a social group would be an adaptive trait. From this there would then have emerged specialised cognitive processes associated with an improved ability to derive the basis of the actions of others in the group. Possessing this ability is referred to as having a "Theory of Mind" (ToM) as its presence endows knowledge of the mental processes of others; that is, that the way they think is similar to our own. ToM is thus a facility to determine to some extent what others think. If you want to deceive someone, or gain precedence over them, then being able to ascertain the way they would respond to certain actions or situations is going to impart an advantage. Being able to "read minds" would be a great advantage in the complex social life of primates. Indeed, current research has provided growing evidence from primate studies that apes regularly employ deception strategies to gain advantages over rivals. Findings by Byrne (1995) and Byrne and Whiten (1991, 1992) show that both gorillas and chimpanzees demonstrate the ability deceive other group members to gain access to food or engage in sexual behaviour prohibited by dominant males. This behaviour provides strong evidence for the existence of a ToM amongst apes. However, although they have this ability it is much less well developed than with humans.

The chains of reasoning about the mental state of others that provide the basis of understanding the way others think have been referred to by the term "orders of intensionality" by Dennett (1988). The concept of an order of intensionality describes the comprehending of the mental state of someone else through varying levels of nested reciprocity. Believing something involves one level of intensionality, and suspecting that someone may believe something involves two orders of intensionality. The nested progression of orders of intensionality can be shown clearly if each stage is indicated by numerical notation. The following statement shows three orders of intensionality; I believe [1] that you think [2] that I believe [3] .... and onwards by way of an infinite progression. Dennett illustrated how complex such chains can become with the following example of eight orders of intensionality; "I suspect that you wonder whether I realise how hard it is for you to be sure that you understand whether I mean to be saying that you can recognise that I can believe ..." (Dennett 1988: 185-186). Being able to cope with high orders of intensionality would clearly be of an advantage to social animals as those best endowed in this regard would be most able to make sense of the actions of other group members, and thus potentially gain important advantages over rivals and competitors. If this is the case, then it would be expected that there would be an evolutionary trend towards to continuing development of ToM amongst primates. However, as yet, there is no clear evidence for the presence of an ability to operate with multiple orders of intensionality amongst modern apes. Dunbar (1996) suggests that chimpanzees may be able to operate with up to four orders of intensionality, but warns that this finding is based on anecdotal evidence. Mithen (1998) claims that at best chimpanzees can cope with only two orders of intensionality. It is generally held to be the case that human beings can cope with up to six orders, though beyond three the numbers of errors starts to rise exponentially (Dunbar 1996). To date, this is as far as these findings take us. ToM and a facility with orders of intensionality have a clear role in enabling interaction in complex social groups, but the way this came about in evolutionary terms is difficult to determine.

What research on ToM and orders of intensionality does achieve is to draw attention to a possible relationship between the evolution of cognition and aspects of early hominid social life. So far attention has been directed towards relationships between cognitive development and the behavioural or environmental context of early hominid life. This new strand of research introduces the possibility of there being other important components in the pathways of human cognitive evolution. The evolution of modern human cognition may in part have arisen from a divergence between hominids and other primates in terms of core characteristics of social interaction such that advances in an ability to understand others became adaptive. A "Machiavellian Intelligence" (Byrne and Whiten 1988) emerged as an adaptive outcome of changes in sociality.

For Robin Dunbar this focus on the importance of social life provided the starting point for a theory of cognitive evolution based upon certain demands of group living. Dunbar has argued that cranial volume increased in response to increases in the average *Homo* group size. As group size increased so to did brain size. Dunbar developed a set of calculations from studies of contemporary primates that enabled him to estimate from fossil remains the likely group size of human ancestors. By way of this method he calculated that Australopithecines would have lived in groups with a mean size of 67 and *H. habilis* in groups containing on average 82 members. Dunbar and his colleague Leslie Aiello calculated that although primate group size increased generally over evolutionary time in response to predation, the greatest increase in size occurred around two million years ago with the appearance of *Homo*. From that point onwards group size increased exponentially until it reached some 150, the size found for modern humans (see Dunbar 1996). The reasons for increases in size are not known. Dunbar (1996) suggested three possible reasons; firstly, where food is irregularly distributed being a member of a large group that shares finds is more a more successful strategy than scavaging individually or from a small social base. Secondly, it may have occurred in response to predation or competition with other human groups. Thirdly, the increase may have stemmed from nomadic behaviour resulting in the occupation of areas with limited food and water resources. Of course, these three reasons are not mutually exclusive. If early humans were nomadic then each of the other two possible explanations would also apply. Periods of scarcity of food and water and encounters with predators and other human competitors would be more likely in strange territories where knowledge of the environment was absent or very limited. Indeed, a scenario whereby each of these three possible explanations did indeed play a part, interactively, in effecting changes in group size would fit well with the idea of human evolution unfolding in a complex nonlinear manner, as discussed above.

Dunbar argues that these changes in group size led to new demands being placed on early human social life. As a social primate humans spend time gossiping, grooming and seeking to outwit competitors in ways similar to any modern ape. In consequence, it was argued, the "grooming" needs of humans would grow alongside that of group size until they became excessive. No primate exceeds 20% of its time grooming, whereas calculations carried out by Aiello and Dunbar (1993) showed that 40% of social time would be required for modern humans. However, empirical data show that the actual figure for modern human groups is around 25% (Dunbar 1996). Given that it is hypothesised that the demands for social grooming remain a fixed function of group size, then something must have happened. The argument is that language evolve as a means to maintain the demands of social grooming without requiring that nearly half of each day be spent in direct physical social interaction. Language, it is argued, evolved as a replacement for the increasing demands on time that resulted from physical social grooming.

Co-evolution and Multi-dimensionality in Human Reasoning

One major conclusion of the above discussion is that despite the speculative nature of some of the issues raised, the evidence suggests that human reasoning is not a one dimensional facility. It has been claimed that evidence from a variety of sources suggests that it was most likely tool manufacture and use which formed the primary basis of the emergence of symbolic reasoning in early hominids. Although later language played an increasing part in the further development of higher-order consciousness, first of all there appeared humankind the problem solver. It is probably the case that subsequent to these early events language and problem solving co-evolved so that eventually the ability to rationalise the external world became a dominant characteristic of humankind. This developed as a continuing processes which ultimately gave rise to science and the creative arts. Nevertheless, the fact that social interaction is a central part of human life cannot be overlooked. It is undoubtably the case language development took place within the framework of a complex society and an emerging cultural life. A cultural life that formed gradually as social life, once driven by instinct and limited learning, became melded to the rationalising influence of higher-order consciousness. This unfolding of cognition by way of separate but interwoven processes promotes a portrayal of cognition as series of nested components. That is, human reasoning can be viewed as a product of the nesting of separate processes and functions which co-evolved over time to produce a complex, multidimensional outcome. In evolutionary terms, human cognition is composite rather than uniform.

A more common way of describing the multi-dimensionality of human cognition is by way of modular theories of the mind. So far it has been argued that human cognition is based on a primary ability to reason symbolically and, later, language. These are given as the key evolutionary moments in the emergence of the mental life of modern humans. This picture is, though, somewhat incomplete because we know already from Cosmides's work that human cognition is also characterised by the presence of Darwinian algorithms, adaptive modules associated with particular types of problem solving. Findings from research on the social intelligence of primates also adds further complexity. In consequence of the complex social life of primates there has developed a Machiavellian intelligence and an ability to "read minds" by way of being able to operate with multiple orders of intensionality. Human beings posses these abilities to a far greater extent than any other primate. Our mental life is thus a complex medium.

Some current research has taken the modular approach through further levels of intricacy and, for example, Gardner (1983) has depicted a mental life comprising elements relating to linguistic, musical, logical, spatial, kinesthetic and personal intelligence. The suggestion is that each of these cognitive modules arose adaptively from the different demands of early hominid life. A Swiss army knife analogy where each cognitive blade arose to serve a particular function (see Mithen 1998). Cosmides and Tooby (1992) pursued a similar approach but include a much more exhaustive range of modules each of which, they argue, arose by way of adaptive processes. Their list includes a face recognition module, a spatial relations module, a tool-use module, an emotion-perception module, a friendship module, and so on. One problem with this approach is its reductionist tendency. Where would one stop when compiling a such a list? As Mithen (1998) has noted, the end result is not too dissimilar from Gardner's when it is recognised that Cosmides's and Tooby's list can be restructured to form modules comprising similar types of mental facilities. The key point is that at some point it is necessary to consider the outcome of the operation of a multitude of "knife blades" or modules. How is the mental life of contemporary human beings formed from these separate moments of of evolutionary past. For Mithen (1998) this occurs by way of integration. People do not access thought through separated cognitive modules but in a holistic way. This suggests a coordinated intellect within which various aspects of mental life are interconnected (Mithen 1998).

In considering human consciousness in this way it becomes apparent that once again we are looking at a complex system which, from the neurological level to that of self-awareness, is a product of the interaction of a very large number of elements of differing character and function. In evolutionary terms this means that the most primal components of our mental life associated with, say, the avoidance of pain and hunger are inter-linked with those of a higher-order, such as algorithms related to social exchange. However, although they are integrated they also can function independently. If modular theories of the mind are to work then they need to incorporate ideas about self-organisation, a component of complexity theory. What self-organisation means is that parts of a complex system can be semi-decomposable. That is, they can function in part as though they were separate systems, but being only semi-decomposable they are also subject to feedback and feed-forward between other self-organising parts of the total system (Lee 1997). Thus the outcome of a self-organising sub-system is primarily the product of its own internal function, but is also the result of inputs and outputs to other parts of the system. It is not too difficult to see how this representation of systemic organisation could be applied to the model of the evolution of human cognition being presented here. Modular components have arisen by way of specific moments of adaptation, but at each stage they are integrated within a broader mental life as self-organising components. Our mental life emerges moment by moment by way of the resolution of the feedback and feed-forward between self-organising cognitive units.

As with other complex systems of large dimensions it may thus be expected that outcomes may not always be predicted. Indeed, rather than human consciousness having reach some advanced stage of formal rationality, is otherwise at one moment primal, at another adaptively rational, then at the next moment formally scientific. As with other complex systems that evolve in a nonlinear way patterns of change are unpredictable. All we can know with certainty is that from moment to moment our cognitive status either stays the same or it changes. Self evidently this would appear to have implications for the way life is experienced both individually and socially. So, in chapter four attention will turn to the consequences of this complexity both in terms of establishing a way to ground these ideas biologically, and with respect to individual and social outcomes.

4 Encountering the Cultural World

The analysis presented above with respect to current findings on the evolution of cognition has argued that the unfolding of its modular basis will follow patterns arising from complex nonlinear systems. Any given state will be an emergent outcome of the great interconnectivity that exists between individual self-organising components (that will in turn arise from deeper levels of interconnectivity). The mind can thus work in an integrated way, but this does not mean that the expression of individual self-organising components (i.e. modules) is suppressed. There will be maintained the potential to produce cognitive outcomes specific to their primary function. The case of Brother John cited in chapter three is but one example of the divisibility of cognitive function into component parts; in that case the separation of language and the appraisal of social interaction. As argued by Mithen (1998), Cosmides and Tooby (1992) and others, each module arises from specific circumstances encountered in our evolutionary past. This means that our mental life unfolds cognitively in a simultaneous way on multiple evolutionary levels. In other words, our cognition is historical. From moment to moment different aspects of our evolutionary past will come to the fore. Cognitively we are not solely modern humans, we are also the Neanderthal or *H.erectus* of our distant past.

In Dean (1997) a distinction was made between aspects of human cognition denoted as instincts, reason, adaptive rationality and formal rationality. The purpose in presenting human cognitive function in those terms was to illustrate that each stage of the evolution of the brain is reflected in particular types of mentation. That is, although historically our hominid past is a long way distant, some aspects of that life are still mirrored in our contemporary lives through the way we perceive the external world and solve problems. Not only in terms of function, as described by the idea of Darwinian algorithms, but also with respect to a hierarchical ordering of sub-systems. What this means is that on some occasions and in some part our actions may be instinctive, whilst at others they may arise from a precise formal calculation of possible outcomes. In addition, it may also be the case that what we do think on any given occasion may be the outcome of several of these aspects of our mental life acting at, or close to, the same moment in time. This argument has significant implications for any consideration of the relationship between human agency and culture. Human agency becomes a problematic concept comprising instincts, reason, adaptive rationality and formal rationality. Both the cultural and the natural world (as represented in specific adaptations to non-human environmental influences) are seen to be represented in the progress of our mental life.

Historical Cognition

According to Plotkin (1994) instincts are species-specific behaviours that are structured within the brain by way of natural selection. These behaviours can be elicited by environmental events outwith conscious intention; such as, for example, defensive or aggressive responses to a physical attack. Reason is a more complex element of cognition to describe than is the case with instincts. In evolutionary terms, reason will have arisen after the development of instinctive responses to the external environment associated with fundamental responses to food, reproduction and defence. In Dean (1997) a simple thought experiment was carried out in which the reader was invited to consider the parameters needed to design a self-replicating creature. The early stages of this thought experiment described as an outcome the creation of a creature that by being able to detect and consume food and water had stabilised its numbers at (an arbitrary) limited population size of 80 individuals. This limitation on population size arose, it was argued, from the presence of predators. Avoiding predation was not easy as it became apparent that simply designing a creature which avoided the approach of any other creature would not work as they would then, in consequence, spend much of their time running away from all moving objects. Neither would it be possible to map to the genotype of the creature a list of all predation events and predators so that it could instinctively avoid predators. There would be far too many possible scenarios for this to be readily achieved. Instead, it was argued, all that would be needed would be to implant a desire to avoid physical damage, set up an in built capability to map and recall those occasions when damage occurred, and link this to an avoidance response. Once these changes were implemented (through a simulated process of evolution) the creature would then be able to categorise perceptual inputs, remember them, collate these with survival-related criteria and emit a behavioural response.

This ability to categorise and recall events in terms of species-specific value criteria has been termed "primary consciousness" by Edelman (1992). For Edelman, primary consciousness is a type of "remembered present", by which is meant the real-time recall of unfolding events. The reader may find it helpful to understand this as a form of déjà vu, the experience of perceiving an event that has already taken place. One explanation of déjà vu which is helpful in developing this current discussion may be made in terms of there being a delay in becoming consciously aware of an event taking place in real-time which has otherwise been processed in short-term memory. The event taking place is received into short-term memory, but it has not been processed consciously. When conscious recognition of the event occurs a brief moment later than the time taken to store it in short-term memory, the perception is that the event has already taken place. We are, of course, usually capable of consciously comparing ongoing events to those stored in memory, so this perceptual delay is disorienting. But for organisms without conscious awareness, a form of "remembering the present" will, according to Edelman, be the principal form of consciousness. In Dean (1997) the cognitive outcome of this form of mentation, of primary consciousness, was termed "reason", to distinguish it from higher-order cognition concerned with forms of symbolic rationality.

In summary, primary consciousness is the outcome of an interconnectiveness between species level values (recall the function of the limbic-brain stem region), perceptual categorisation, memory and the emitting of certain behaviours. That is, primary consciousness is concerned with adaptive learning in the absence of self-conscious awareness. In this sense primary consciousness is involved with value-based learning, and thus actions which arise from this can arguably be designated "reasoned" actions; the product of a species-level Reason. There will be a strong desire to undertake reasoned actions, but unlike instinctual behaviour, reasoned action arises through learning about the environment. It is the basis of thought or action directed towards an intended outcome but absent of any symbolisation and self-awareness.

Adaptive rationality was discussed in some detail in chapter three, where it was argued that natural selection, operating within the context of a linguistic, collective social life, has given rise to Darwinian cognitive algorithms. As the reader will recall, these algorithms are adaptations to cognition concerned with deductive reasoning. In addition to possessing abilities in formal logic, in tests of logic concerned with rule testing, it has been found by Cosmides and others that people operate according to social rules, and that in certain circumstances an "adaptive" logic has precedence over formal logic. Unlike the "Reason" associated with primary consciousness, adaptive rationality is consequently a property of social interaction. It has to do with how people interact in social circumstances to safeguard against individual disadvantage. Or in less teleological terms, natural selection has given rise to adaptations in cognition that function to enhance the survival or reproductive chances of the individual within social environments. Other examples from research on a Theory of Mind, orders of intensionality and the presence of a Machiavellian intelligence were also cited. Each of these aspects of human mental life can also be considered to be aspects of an adapted rationality in that their functioning does not depend on any conscious awareness. As with the "logic of social exchange" what is being addressed is a cognitive ability rather than the expression of a conscious intention to solve a particular type of problem (as would be the case in solving an abstract mathematical or philosophical problem). The case of autism may make this point somewhat clearer. Autistic people display severe difficulties in engaging in social interaction. This dysfunction is believed to result from an impairment in that aspect of cognition concerned with the execution of a Theory of Mind (ToM). In all other respects autistic people exhibit normative levels of mental performance, they just do not seem to be able to work out what other people are thinking. For autistic people the problem is that there seems to be missing a crucial cognitive module. They are unable even to think about the mental life of others, hence for them there can be no conscious intention to seek to determine why others act as they do. As it is held that ToM is an adaptive cognitive module associate with determining the way others think (and is thus an aspect of an adaptive rationality) it follows that the concept of an adaptive rationality refers to certain mental abilities rather than intended computations.

Formal Rationality and the Integration of Mind

The emergence of a composite mind of adaptive modules was not the end point for the evolution of human cognition. At some stage in our evolutionary history a level of integration between modules was achieved such that the ability to analyse and represent the external world symbolically gave rise to the ability to think creatively about the external world. This then led to an expansion of rationality to included the framing of laws about the physical world, and a formal rationality arose. Over time this would have led to a form of logical analysis which was qualitatively different from the adaptive foci of Darwinian algorithms. The possibility that the formal mental life of modern humans arose from the integration of evolutionarily distinct cognitive modules was suggested by Mithen (1998), and is similar to that developed by Edelman (1992) regarding the development of higher-order consciousness. Recall that Edelman argued that mind comes into being by way of the increasing integration of distinct areas of the brain that fulfil particular functions. Over evolutionary time and by way of developmental processes, different areas of the brain become linked through reentrant connectiveness and the resultant formation of neural maps, and ultimately the foundation of global maps (see chapter two). Now, it can be seen that these are a series of statements about physiological development that chart well with Mithen's ideas about the integration of cognitive modules (that in turn are in part a reflection of Cosmides's and Tooby's ideas about Darwinian algorithms). A cognitive module (Darwinian algorithm) is a neural map that has arisen in a specific functional form adaptively, and finds a specific, personal expression through developmental processes in childhood. The cognitive integration of modules occurs through the formation of global maps (and even meta-global maps) as an outcome of both evolutionary and developmental processes. The integration of modules occurs by way of the formation of (meta) global maps historically and during childhood development, and it is these processes that gave rise to our higher-order consciousness.

For Edelman (1992) higher-order consciousness comes into being through acquiring an ability to interact with the external world symbolically. This occurs by way of the generation of abstract symbols about the present which can be remembered and used to reflect on future events. Within Edelman's analysis, symbolisation was associated with the emergence of language through the sharing of meanings ascribed to phonological sounds. Thus, he argued, higher-order consciousness was always a collective, linguistic aspect of cognition. As discussed above, in this present analysis it was contended that early symbolic reasoning arose by way of tool manufacture and use, and that this gave rise initially to *humankind the problem-solver* prior to *humankind the speechmaker*. Linking this now to the findings of Cosmides (1989), Edelman (1992), Dunbar (1996) and Mithen (1998) it can be seen that it is not possible to separate out from other events in the evolution of cognition those that were primarily the cause of the formation of formal rationality and self-conscious awareness. This arose at some unknowable point in human evolution as the emergent outcome of an increasing interconnectiveness between phylogenically distinct categories of mind.

Initially our most distant ancestors, in common with many other animals, were guided by nothing more than instinctive responses to external stimuli. These response were based on species-level values concerned with food, safety and reproduction. Next came a primary consciousness which, from the inter-linking of improved perceptual responses and memory (see chapter two), moderated instincts by the means of learning. Primary consciousness led to the establishment of a flexible response to a wide-range of external stimuli. The need for each circumstance being preset at birth became unnecessary. Limited responses could thus have been made on an individual basis to changes in the environment. Species-level constraints on action would have still been highly prescribed, as is the case with contemporary animals other than humankind (lions do not suddenly start building shelters), but flexibility in response became possible. At that point in our evolutionary history the wide-scale proliferation of neural maps (as proposed by Edelman) could have formed the physiological basis for the emergence of distinct cognitive modules or Darwinian algorithms. Cognitive evolution would then have proceeded through continuing feedback and feed-forward between mind and an increasingly intricate social life. Different selective circumstances would have given rise to a range of semi-autonomous cognitive proficiencies until at some point a form of integration arose adaptively that gave rise to self-conscious awareness and a formal rationality. Language would have played a key role in the process.

Language and Self-consciousness

It is most likely that the evolution of language was driven more by social and cultural events than natural selection acting through the physical environment. The evolution of many aspects of mind, such as a tool-making ability, can be readily understood as occurring by way of selective pressures acting non-socially at the individual level. However, the emergence of categories of cognition of a more collective nature can perhaps best be seen as an outcome of social interaction. The appearance of a "speaking" hominid is most likely to have happened in response to changing demands of social living. This is the point made by Dunbar in his analysis of the role of grooming in the evolution of the mind. Dunbar may well be correct, or perhaps language initially stemmed from a cross-over between a symbolic ability founded on tool-making and primitive vocalisations. Access to language and the consequent sharing of symbols about the external environment may have increased the capacity of a prior "natural history intelligence" (see Mithen 1998). This may then have engendered the expansion of food-seeking into new, larger territories. Larger territories would have meant larger groups (as argued by Dunbar) and this would then have led to increasing demands on grooming, which would in turn have led to further selective pressure on language. Given the complex, emergent nature of human cognition being argued for here, it is unlikely that we will ever know the actual course of these events. However, it is reasonable to assume that once language emerged the subsequent evolution of hominid cognitive abilities would have been driven largely by such social and cultural forces.

The mental life of a modern human is the outcome of integration between semi-decomposable cognitive modules, each the outcome of distinct adaptive moments in our evolutionary past. This integration is facilitated through language by way of a self-conscious appreciation of the "self". Clearly our mental life functions subconsciously as well as consciously, this has been widely known to be the case from Freud onwards, but our formal rationality is orchestrated through our conscious mentation, the knowing "I". This orchestration of cognition on the basis of "I" could not have occurred except by way of collective action. Self-consciousness awareness did not arise as a necessary end product of the development of symbolic reasoning but by way of language, itself an adaptation to a collective, symbolic social life.

Once language emerged, its use spread from the primal demands of a hominid social life to include everything that could be perceived. The world became the property of language and humankind the problem-solver set about naming and disclosing on the physical and social world. Through communicating with others on the nature of the world a sense of personal being arose; a conscious identification that "I" was separate from "it" and from "you". Self-conscious awareness grew from an expanding symbolic categorisation of the world to include recognition of individual agency in causal chains - if "that" happens then "I" experience "this", and if "I" do that then "this" takes place. Events could be imagined as well as experienced, and outcomes could then be considered in relation to a "self". A ToM is part of this process, but its realisation also required the ability to construct symbolic ideas about the product of orders of intensionality. Language meant that they could be named, categorised and rendered in novel ways. It became possible to contemplate the nature of death, but also to construct through creative reflection and imagination almost infinite possibilities for future action. There emerged a comprehension of a past, present and future, and an understanding of the implications of actions for the self and for the social group.

Complex Mind, Complex World

An analysis of just when in human history these distinct events in the evolution of cognitive took place is beyond this current analysis. The purpose here has been to show that human intelligence cannot be viewed as a type of uniform computer, but is instead a composite adaptive organ featuring high levels of functional integration. The evolutionary path that led to the development of human self-consciousness and formal rationality was thus complex and discontinuous. Our cognitive abilities are multidimensional. Although we can still act instinctively, at other times our actions are guided by the reason of primary consciousness, sometimes through an adaptive rationality and at yet others consciously by way of a formal logic. This means that human cognitive outcomes emerge within a complex system of conscious and subconscious thought that is the product of adaptive forces within both the natural environment and the social environment. Human reasoning has evolved discontinuously in response to adaptive forces of both a natural and social form.

Discontinuity in Mental Life

The idea that human consciousness is not only modular but also hierarchically structured (in terms of there being instincts, reason, adaptive rationality and formal rationality) is not new. Although directed towards issues different from those of this current analysis, Maslow's hierarchy of needs also drew attention to the layering of elements in human cognition, the simultaneous existence primal needs associated with hunger and thirst, as well as higher-order interests related to creativity and the fulfilment of personal goals. These different aspects are mirrored in this current analysis in that primal needs are referred to here as instincts associated with limbic-brain stem function, and creativity and notions of the "self" with higher-order consciousness.

However, as important as Maslow's works was, his depiction of human consciousness was based on a hierarchy of needs that suggested a linear progression in conscious or sub-conscious thought. Having "satisfied" one level of "need" progression could then be made to another level. Here a related point is being made quite differently. Although it is being argued that human mental life is formed from the hierarchical integration of modular elements, this does not mean that cognition functions in some orderly and sequential way. When a person feels hungry they they may still think about other things, either consciously or subconsciously, and when feeling fearful of some unfolding event people are capable of a range of different response. Being reduced to total inaction is but one of these responses. In the midst of combat people are capable of both great compassion and terrible cruelty. Often we are unaware of what our response will be until something actually happens to us. For example, a relationship may be coming to an end and the people involved may feel great anxiety, but they often will not have been able to anticipate the thoughts and feelings they will have once the parting has taken place. They may unexpectedly find themselves feeling elated, but equally they may otherwise feel very depressed.

Why should this be the case? One would perhaps reasonably expect that as certain aspects of the human mind evolved by way of natural selection to mirror closely the demands of a human social life, it would be mapped directly to those demands, in much the same way as the hunting strategy of a cheetah is mapped to the escape strategies of a gazelle. Well, in most respects the human mind is closely mapped to the social and other conditions that comprise the environment within which humankind cognition evolved, but these conditions are not linear in the sense that simple rules of causality apply. Our mental life arises as a consequence of the activity present in each of the individual modular elements that comprise the mind. Although each of these has a partial independence of function, they are almost completely decomposable, each is also linked by way of feedback and feed-forward to all of the others. The integration of functions that has been referred to above is achieved through the interconnection of modules, and the hierarchical structure derives from the evolutionary development of sub-systems of interconnectivity. The outcome of this integrated, meta-interconnectivity is our self-conscious mind. Our self-consciousness is thus an emergent outcome of this interconnectivity.

Of course this does not mean that we can think anything, we are constrained ultimately by species level conditions that are a reflection of our evolutionary past. Recall that our mind is composed of elements that arose adaptively. As discussed in chapter two, although the state of a complex system comprising many interacting parts cannot be predicted from one time interval to the next, change is still restricted to certain species level conditions (there is order as well as chaos in complex systems). Although the strange attractor that defines the path of evolution of such a system may be infinitely long, it is contained within a finite dimension. Although variation within a complex system may be wide, the range of possible changes is constrained by the nature of the system. In the biological world the dimensions of a system are designated by species level constraints. Here it is being argued that the same condition applies to our mental life. We can think extraordinary things, but we can only think human things. Our mind is a reflection of our evolutionary past in that adaptive moments from the pre-history of modern humans are reflected in some way in each and every thinking moment. It could not be other than this given that our mental life is an emergent outcome of our evolutionary past.

The Co-evolution of Cognition and Culture

Deacon (1997) has argued that people learn languages easily not because they possess a "language instinct' comprising the means to resolve grammatical structures, but because human consciousness and languages have co-evolved. That is, we have the types of language we do have because they are easy for children to learn, and we have the type of brain we have because it is good at language-related symbolic reasoning. Notwithstanding the difference between Deacon's analysis and the discussion presented in this book regarding the genesis of these events, this is a convincing argument. Similarly, therefore, it can also be argued that the evolution of other cognitive facilities also co-evolved in relation to changes in the environment.

One thing that distinguishes humankind from other primates is that to a far greater extent than any other species humankind is capable of effecting intended changes to their environment. In consequence, human social and cultural activity has led to adaptive change. An example of this process was given in chapter one with respect to the farming practices of the Kwa speaking people of West Africa and the subsequent rise in the population of malarial carrying mosquitoes (Durham 1991). In this sense human evolution is not just a process driven by the natural world, nor is it solely a response to changes in social behaviour. Over time human evolution has been less affected by the natural and social behavioural environment than by human culture. Historically early hominids functioned by way of instincts and primary consciousness. Over time diverse influences led to the development of a modularised intelligence and the emergence of an adaptive rationality concerned with social life. Some of these changes took place adaptively in response to natural environmental conditions, whereas others arose in response to social behavioural pressures, as previously discussed. At some point there emerged a formal rationality direct towards the systematic examination of the external social and physical world. At this point humankind began to intentionally change their environment through conscious activity. As has been described above, such changes affected the extent and nature of environmental selective pressure. Increasingly, cultural action defined the context of human evolution. A system of feedback and feed-forward between nature, culture and cognition arose. This process of feedback and feed-forward led to the establishment of continuous iterations between cultural change and adaptive change. Eventually social, cultural and cognitive life became established in a pattern of co-evolution permeated throughout by the external, natural world.

Human cultural practices did not arise within a vacuum, but were instead grounded in material concerns related to reproduction, the acquisition of food and shelter, and the avoidance of predators and other natural hazards. As has been argued, these external conditions are the property of naturally occurring systems that possess certain endemic characteristics of change associated with order and chaotic behaviour. The world we inhabit, and within which our ancestors originated, is itself changing according to the rules of complex nonlinear systems. In consequence, when human life adapted to its external environment it developed behaviours and ways of reasoning which were based upon the comprehension of nonlinear change. And as a social life based upon language and symbolic reasoning developed, ways of relating to a complex world of order and chaos were collectively enshrined both cognitively and behaviourally in cultural practices. As a result of these processes cultural life has not developed beyond nature, in fact the opposite is true. Our cultural life, although increasingly invested with the concerns and issues which stem from the practice of techniques derived from formal rationality, is still in many regards a reflection of the complex nature-culture world from which it emerged in the distant past. Humankind is still both cognitively and culturally bound by the substance of the natural world, either through the biological embodiment of our mind (in both physiological and evolutionary terms) or in terms of the continued presence of environmental constraints. Although there are moments when through abstract reasoning human life may indeed transcend nature, in general nature and culture remain indivisible. Human cultural and mental life is still bonded to the natural world. What this means is that cultural practices are themselves the emergent outcome of an enduring interconnectivity between cognition and nature. In the next chapter the biosocial context of incest taboos will be used as a case-study to illustrate this point.

5 Nature in Culture

The question of the relationship between human culture and nature is an enduring one within the social sciences and philosophy. There are those too numerous to list who see culture as transcending nature, of being the main driving force in the day to day life of modern human. It is frequently asserted directly or by implication, particularly within postmodern social science, that culture has become the primary force in human life. Natural selection has become become cultural selection. Since the emergence within social science of paradigms concerned with the subjective world of humankind and the role of language and communication in defining the quality and experience of social life (beginning primarily with the German Idealists and the Frankfurt School), there has developed a view of human life which places at the dominant centre discursive practices and unstructured, diverse cultural practices. There are others, however, who have argued differently and claimed that much of human social and personal life is still determined by nature through our biological structure and environmental constraints. Attempts to uncover the biological basis of sexual preference or predispositions towards the use of intoxicants provide two examples of biologically-led contemporary research into areas of human action which others would claim are the product solely of cultural influences.

In between these two extremes, drawn here for the sake of illustration, stand those who argue that nature and culture are indivisibly part of human life; both nature and culture give rise to human personal experience and social life. Although this aspect of his work is infrequently commented on, the broad work of Marx falls into this category. One of Marx's main concerns was to transcend the nature-culture dichotomy which existed in philosophy and social science during his time. For Marx one essential aspect of the human condition was that it derived ultimately from material conditions, not from social life or subjective experience. All that humankind creates is a product of the material world. From conditions set by the material world there emerged a mind that gave rise to art, science, law and politics. For Marx thoughts were the direct product of material processes. Human mental life was enclosed by material preconditions. The central tenet of Marx's philosophy held that the material conditions of human existence gave rise to consciousness. This basic concept was developed further into a theory of dialectical materialism.

Dialectical materialism stood in opposition to the dominant perspectives in science at that time (and which still continue in many branches of science) that were directed towards explanations based upon gradual change. Dialectics is concerned with rapid change from one state to another, and thus dialectical materialism is based on the idea of there being rapid change in human affairs stemming from the material basis of human existence.

It is not the intention here to delve further into Marxist theory, the purpose in drawing attention to his work here has been to illustrate that within social science there have been continuing endeavours to situate humankind and human social life within rather than apart from nature. Although Marx's work stands as a significant achievement in this regard there are contemporary writers who pursue the same objective, if by different means. The work of Giddens and Latour comes readily to mind. However, further discussion of these and other contributions will be postponed until the next chapter when the analysis being presented in this current book will used to critique current subjectivist and postmodern approaches in the social sciences. Indeed the reader may have already perceived the beginnings of such a critique in the brief preamble to this current chapter.

Concerns relating to the material basis of consciousness and the presence of rapid and discontinuous change in human affairs that lie at the centre of Marx's dialectical materialism are echoed in this current text. For now, though, the intention is to draw the dialogue towards a substantive discussion of the analysis presented in previous chapters. It has been argued that human cognition is the emergent outcome of the unfolding of multiple adaptive moments, and that from this there has arisen a discontinuous, multidimensional consciousness. Our present day mental life mirrors both the historical and contemporary conditions of our material, social and cultural life. Mind, society and nature are inextricably linked.

If this is so, then it will be possible to disclose on certain aspects of human social life which reflect directly the enduring existence of nature in human action. To develop this argument substantively an analysis of incest taboos will be presented. The phenomenon of incest is a particularly appropriate subject for the current analysis due to the widespread differences of opinion the subject has engendered. From one time to another both biological and cultural antecedents have been argued for in a mutually exclusive manner. Conversely there have been analyses that have adopted some form of biosocial view, seeing the importance of both biology and culture in the formation of incest taboos. It is this latter approach that will be adopted here. In the succeeding discussion it will be argued that the practice of incest and the substance of incest proscriptions provides good substantive evidence for the indivisibility of nature and culture in human affairs.

Incest, and the Embedding of Nature in Culture

From the late 1800s onwards there has been considerable interest in establishing the origins of prohibitions on incest. But despite having attracted the attention of some of the most prominent anthropologists of the last 100 hundred years, there is still little agreement over the emergent conditions of taboos on sexual acts between consanguineous kin. As will be readily understood from earlier discussion in this present book, any search for the origins of any aspect of human endeavour is encumbered by many problems. From a Darwinian perspective it is necessary to surmise from an adaptationist perspective and deduce the circumstances from which such a prohibition would impart a survival advantage. From a social anthropological stance it is necessary to provide evidence of cultural advantage or enhancement for any proposed theory. Over the years these and other perspectives have provided a considerable number of insights into the prohibition of close inbreeding, but as yet there is no consensus on either the origin or purpose of the incest taboo. In fact the term itself has different meanings for different societies as, although taboos on incestuous relationships are universal, the interpretation of incest varies from one society to the next. This being so, the incest taboo in any given society can be best considered to be a set of restrictions that limit heterosexual acts between categories of kin (Aberle et. al. 1968).

Clearly this lack of any universality in form is highly problematic. In one respect a universal characteristic of humankind is being addressed, and yet in other respects different behaviours are involved. In addition, it should be recognised that a distinction needs to be made between origin and function. From a biological anthropological perspective we need only be concerned with the origins of incest taboos, as was the case with respect to the earlier discussion of the emergence of tool-making and language. However, from a sociological or social anthropological point of view it is necessary that the function of incest taboos also be considered. Only by making such distinctions can both the universal and culturally diversified nature of incest be resolved.

Westermarck (1894) probably stands alone in being the only

writer of his time to discuss both the origins and function of incest. For Westermarck incest prohibition emerged from sexual indifference or revulsion towards those sharing the early childhood environment, and its function was to prevent inbreeding. As will be discussed later in this chapter, Westermarck's analysis is not without shortcomings, but nevertheless his focus on origins and function provides a template for this current discussion. It indeed must be the case that the origin and continuing purpose of incest taboos stem from different causes. Originally, the avoidance of inbreeding will almost certainly have arisen adaptively through natural selection acting directly through the appearance of lethal traits arising from genetic recombination. The reason for this is straightforward. So perhaps this is the best starting point. Firstly, biological aspects of inbreeding will be considered, and this will be followed by an analysis of the social and cultural context of incest. Finally, the extent to which incest can be seen to be an example of the embedding of nature in culture will be considered.

Biology, Natural Selection and Inbreeding

Predictions of deleterious outcomes from inbreeding stem from basic genetic theory. Each gene has two distinct forms known as alleles. Alleles can be dominant or recessive. Dominant alleles are always expressed if they are present in the genome, whereas recessive genes are only expressed if they are expressed by both alleles. During sexual reproduction offspring will receive one allele from the male parent and one allele from the female parent (hence each parent contributes 50% to the offspring genome). If both parents are heterozygous for a particular gene (that is, they carry both dominant and recessive alleles of a given gene) then their offspring will have a 50% chance of being heterozygous for that gene, 25% chance of being homozygous for the dominant gene and 25% chance of being homozygous for the recessive gene. The following example will illustrate these outcomes of recombination resulting from sexual reproduction. Both the female and the male parent carries a dominant and a recessive allele of the gene for eye colour. The allele for brown eyes is dominant whereas the allele for blue eye colour is recessive, in consequence both parents will have brown eyes. However, through the recombination of these alleles that takes place during sexual reproduction the offspring of these two parents will have a 75% chance of having brown eyes and a 25% chance of having blue eyes. This outcome occurs in the following way: if the dominant allele is represented by "S" and the recessive by "s" and they recombine during reproduction at random then the outcome is Ss x Ss = 0.25 SS, 0.25 ss and 0.5 Ss. As only ss would give rise to blue eyes the distribution of eye colour is biased towards brown eyes. Now, if eight children were born to these parents the expected distribution of eye colour would lead to there being six children with brown eyes and two with blue eyes.

Obviously in this example there are no deleterious outcomes arising from this situation. However, if the alleles "S" and "s" did not represent eye colour, but instead a harmful or lethal condition, then homozygosity for recessive genes would need to be avoided. The prevalence of such a deleterious trait could not be known routinely as it would only become apparent through its effect when a person carrying a recessive allele mated with another person who also carried the allele. However, in natural populations it could be expected that harmful or lethal alleles of health-related genes would be rare, as those who inherited them may fail to thrive and may thus be less likely to reach reproductive age (i.e. prereproductive mortality could be high). However, as the harmful recessive allele of the health-related gene would not be expressed in a heterozygous state, it would persist within originating population (those heterozygous for the trait would continue to pass it on within the population). If outbreeding took place then the recessive allele would be passed to other gene pools, but, as the homozygous condition would be even more rare than would be the case within the originating population, it would be seldom, if ever, expressed. The more widespread the outbreeding then the lower would be the frequency of expression of the lethal trait.

If outbreeding did occur on a widespread basis it would be expected that eventually the recessive allele would be established within all overlapping gene pools. Nevertheless, the resultant frequency of occurrence of the trait coded for by the recessive allele would be low within such an extended outbreeding population. Consequently, it would be expected that homozygosity for the recessive trait would be very rare (mating between a couple heterozygous for the deleterious trait would be infrequent). However, in these circumstances *inbreeding* remains problematic. If one parent carried the harmful recessive allele but the other parent did not, so there was a Aa AA cross, then the outcome would be 50% homozygosity for the dominant allele (AA) and 50% probability of heterozygosity (Aa). Therefore none of their offspring would suffer congenital defects from this gene. If, however, two siblings from this union mated there would then be a 12.5% chance of homozygosity for the recessive trait (the probability of an Aa x Aa cross is 50%). Hence, with sibling inbreeding where one parent carries a recessive trait there is a vastly increased chance of homozygosity for the deleterious allele, and thus the occurrence of a harmful congenital condition. For this reason it is reasonable to expect that close inbreeding within gene pools where there are present deleterious recessive traits would be selected against during natural selection. Where close inbreeding was practised there would be expected to be high levels of prereproductive mortality. In essence, natural selection would be acting to reduce such practices as close inbreeding would prove to be an unsuccessful reproductive strategy.

Over recent years there has been a variety of research carried out on different groups of people to establish whether or not contemporary inbreeding does give rise to either increased mortality or other negative health effects. Findings show that even first cousin marriages can give rise to negative health outcomes. One measure of the effects of inbreeding is the impact on anthropometric measures such as stature and height. Krishan (1986) found evidence of a slight inbreeding depression for eight anthropometric measurements amongst the Sheikh Sunni Muslim boys of Delhi. There were found to be reductions with respect to stature, span, sitting height, head length, head circumference, chest girth and calf circumference. Shami et al (1991) in reporting on the effects of consanguinity on 662 babies delivered in Lahore, Pakistan found a relative decline in birth weight, recumbent length, head circumference and chest girth. They also found a reduction in gestational period. However, Khlat (1989) reported an absence of a significant pattern in the relationship between consanguinity and prematurity, weight, length, head circumference and chest circumference.

In addition to anthropometric effects of inbreeding, many studies have investigated more direct negative health-related outcomes. Khoury et al (1987) reviewed 31 studies with 294 observations that compared infant and child mortality amongst offspring of unrelated parents with offspring of first cousin, first cousin once removed and second cousin marriages. They found that the attributable risk of prereproductive mortality due to consanguineous marriages was less than 5%. However, they also found that countries with rates of consanguineous marriages greater than 5% had lower median relative risks than did countries with lower consanguineous rates. Other studies have also shown a lack of a correlation between consanguineous marriage and negative health outcomes. Saha et al (1990) reported that from a study of 4,471 pregnancy outcomes in a Sudanese population that analysed rates of abortions, physical deformity, mental retardation and other congenital abnormalities, no significant difference in reproductive loss or net fertility was observed to exist between inbred and outbred groups. However they did find a significantly higher rate of childhood deaths with inbred marriages.

Other studies have found that inbreeding does not always lead to negative outcomes on all measures for all groups. Reddy (1992) detailed results from research carried out on the inbreeding effects on reproductive outcomes of 2078 women of the Vadde fishing population of Kolleru Lake, Andhra Pradesh, India. Reddy concluded that the results were comparable to those found for other southern Indian and non-Indian populations in that effects were indiscernible and non-significant. These results are consistent with those of Edmond and De Braekeleer (1993) who found that inbreeding had a minor impact on prereproductive mortality within 251 marriages between first cousins and 258 marriages between first cousins once removed from Saguenay-Lac-Saint-Jean, Quebec, Canada. These authors also found that fertility and primary sterility within these groups and five marriages between uncle and nieces were also unaffected (Edmond and De Braekeleer 1993). A finding supported by Sivakumaran and Karthikeyan (1997) who reported a nonsignificant relationship between inbreeding and reproductive losses amongst the Kota tribe, of the Nilgiri district, Tamil State, India. And al-Abdulkareem and Ballal (1998) found no significant effects of consanguinity on mean birth weight, inherited disease and reproductive wastage amongst 1307 ever-married Saudis surveyed in Dammam city, Eastern Province Saudi Arabia (a rate of 52% consanguineous marriages were reported, and of these 39.3% were first cousin marriages).

The majority of the findings reported so far reveal that consanguineous marriages do not appear to give rise to the negative effects commonly claimed for inbreeding. However, these findings need to be interpreted with caution as populations that have experienced a long history of inbreeding have been found to show lower rates of certain negative outcomes than those where inbreeding has in the past been less common (Savakumaran and Karthikeyan 1997; Reddy 1992; Khlat 1989). And, notwithstanding these findings, research has revealed many occurrences of harm stemming from consanguineous reproduction. Khoury et al (1987) found that about 40% of all prereproductive deaths amongst the present population of the Old Order Amish of Lancaster County, Pennsylvania, USA could be accounted for by inbreeding. Other research directed by Khoury found that the noted levels of prereproductive mortality stemmed from the risk of intrauterine growth retardation and congenital malformations (Khoury et al 1987). A correlation between congenital malformations and consanguineous marriages was found by Jain et al (1993) who reported that the frequency of inbreeding was significant for autosomal recessive disorders, congenital heart disease, multiple malformations, neurological malformations, chromosomal disorders, genitourinary disorders and mental retardation-developmental disorders amongst a clinical population in Pondicherry, South India (400 children with existing congenital disorders were studied with regard to the consanguinity of their parents). Hoodfar and Teebi (1996) found that within a population of Middle Eastern origin sampled at a Clinical genetics Unit in Montreal, autosomal recessive disorders were twice as common amongst the inbred sub-sample than in the outbred sub-sample. Although Abdulrazzaq et al (1997) did not find any significant correlation between consanguinity and reproductive wastage in a sample of 2200 women from Dubai an Al Ain, United Arab Emirates, the children of consanguineous unions did have higher rates of malignancies, congenital abnormalities, mental retardation and "physical handicap". Significant effects with respect to "mental handicap" were also found by Jancar and Johnson (1990).

Taken together these data provide a complex picture of the relationship between consanguinity and negative health outcomes. There appears to be no simple association between consanguineous mating and the negatives outcomes often reported as a key reason for inbreeding to have been selected against during the evolution of humankind, and many other animals. However, caution is needed in the interpretation of these findings as upon closer examination differences in circumstances between dissimilar populations can qualify in important ways distinctions between groups in terms of outcomes. In general, inbreeding in the above cited studies refers to first cousin mating in the majority of cases, where the degree of genetic similarity is much lower than with siblings or parents. In addition, although negative outcomes often do not arise with respect to reproductive outcomes with such mating (such as pregnancy rates or reproductive wastage), autosomal recessive disorders or other congenital disorders tend to occur more frequently from consanguineous mating with first cousins than with respect to non-consanguineous mating. Even in cases where reproductive outcomes are no less problematic from consanguineous mating than in other cases, non-genetic causes may affect such outcomes, such as the increase in gross fertility noted for consanguinity by Bittles et al (1991), which, they argue, is a result in part of the younger maternal age at first live birth associated with such mating in many regions of Asia and Africa. (This is an interesting finding which leads to speculation as to whether there is often a coercive element to consanguineous mating. For there to be differences with respect to age suggests that some form of mistreatment may be involved.) And within those groups where outcomes do not show differences between consanguineous and non-consanguineous mating, a history of long term inbreeding may be the cause, as noted above. In populations where inbreeding has been long established selective forces may have reduced over time the incidence of lethal or extremely harmful recessive traits such that further inbreeding carried a reduced risk.

One important finding to be drawn from the above data is that notwithstanding the risks, inbreeding between close relatives is still practised routinely within many societies, hence incest taboos do not correlate directly with the negative biological outcomes of inbreeding. They must thus serve other social or cultural purposes and inbreeding must be a preferred option when outbreeding is not possible. Generally, the basic purpose of reproduction is to produce related offspring. Hence any action which reduces this possibility will not be favoured over those which do not, even if there is some corresponding risk.

Gains and Losses in Inbreeding and Outbreeding

Shepher (1983) provided a good illustration of the outcomes of inbreeding between close kin in terms of the negative and positive outcomes of such unions. He demonstrated that close inbreeding only provides advantage when outbreeding is not possible. For example, if a brother and sister inbreed when both have the opportunity to outbreed then both will lose out in terms of the number of offspring produced who are related to them genetically. From the brother's perspective he gains from inbreeding in that the offspring he and his sister produce will be more genetically related than if they outbreed, but overall they will both lose the nieces and nephews they would have, in addition to their own offspring, if they had chosen to outbreed. If they had outbred then they would have children from their own mating plus there would be consanguine relationships with the offspring of their siblings. If they inbreed they will only have the offspring from the reproductive act carried out with each other.

Similarly, if a father mates with a daughter he only gains if another mate is not available. If he mates twice through outbreeding then he gains grandchildren by way of the lines of descent from both his outbreeding partners, whereas if he mates once through outbreeding and once with his daughter then he gains only four grandchildren (his children from his daughter will also be his grandchildren). For example, if each union for each generation produces two offspring then through outbreeding with two partners the father gains grandchildren from two mates who each produce two children, who then in turn produce two (grand)children; that is, eight descendents in the second generation. If under the same conditions of only producing two children the father mates with his daughter, then only four grandchildren arise. Hence both the father and the daughter lose in numbers of related kin when outbreeding is a possibility. With mother-son reproduction both lose out as, given once again a finite limit on the number of births possible for any one female, the mother will forfeit a number of grandchildren and the son will forfeit the extra children he would have fathered if he had outbred with a mate that had not already had children by another father. From this analysis Shepher (1983) concluded that inbreeding is disadvantageous when outbreeding is a possibility. It is only successful in genetic terms in cases of isolation and lack of outbreeding possibilities.

However, despite the disadvantages associated with incest in conditions of non-isolation, Shepher (1983) also described circumstances whereby incest may impart advantage, even in conditions which were not markedly isolated. Shepher argued that mating with a stranger involves risk as little would be known about either their genetic well-being (whether or not they carry lethal or damaging genes) or their abilities and commitment to parenting. In this sense mating with someone for whom there is knowledge regarding these factors could be beneficial it terms of promoting successful procreation. As Van den Burghe (1979) has reported, the majority of forms of mating that arise culturally (that is by way of descent rules, residence rules and/or preferential cousin marriages) denote institutions that are directed at promoting inbreeding where it is possible (reported in Shepher 1983). It has also been argued by Shepher (1983) that inbreeding reduces competition for mates when few are available due to geographic or other constraints. In such circumstances it is in the groups interest for agreements to arise regarding first and second cousin marriages.

Given that there are both advantages and disadvantages associated with inbreeding it will have been the case that during the process of evolution the best possible balance between inbreeding and outbreeding would have arisen for each set of circumstances. Groups which were very isolated would have been more disposed towards inbreeding than those where outbreeding was more easily achieved. In consequence, for each set of circumstances there would have been an optimum balance arrived at between inbreeding and outbreeding. Shepher (1983) estimated the costs of inbreeding and outbreeding in terms of gains and losses associated with each strategy where outbreeding entails the risk of the outbreeder not surviving the quest for a mate (being away from the home group entails encountering possibly fatal hazards). By calculating the relative outcome of inbreeding between siblings as opposed to outbreeding in terms of the probability progeny will fail to thrive, the probability that the outbreeder will not survive and the number of children which will result from any union, Shepher (1983) concluded that inbreeding would be the preferred option only if the cost of outbreeding were 1.5 times the cost of inbreeding (that is, where there was a 66% chance that the outbreeder will die). Clearly such conditions would be exceptional, therefore in nearly all circumstances outbreeding would be a more successful outcome. However, as the degree of consanguinity decreases the cost calculated will change. The benefits associated with inbreeding will mean that at some point in the scale of relatedness inbreeding would be a preferred option. Van den Burghe (1979) concluded that in situations where the cost of outbreeding are high, as in the case of small non-stratified groups, first cousin marriages will be prescribed culturally. However, this would would need to be restricted in practice if adverse genetic outcomes are to be limited. Kundstadter et. al. (1964) found that matrilineal cross-cousin marriages cannot exceed between 27% to 28% of all marriages (quoted in Shepher 1983).

The conclusion Shepher (1983) draws from this analysis is that if it is found that actual behaviour conforms to these circumstances relating to the avoidance of damaging inbreeding, then incest prohibitions serve to prevent inbreeding between relatives who share around 50% of their genes. Hence it is expected that it would be easier to find cases involving relatively distant relations such as those represented by first cousin and uncle-niece mating than between genetically closer consanguineous kin.

Recent studies confirm this pattern of mating. Yaqoob et al (1993) found in a study of 940 families from in or around Lahore, Pakistan a prevalence of 46% for consanguineous marriages, the majority of which (67%) were between first cousins, and 19% of which were between second cousins. The rate of consanguineous mating in north Jordan was found to be 63.7% by Alsalem and Rawashdeh (1993), of which 58.5% were between first cousins. Those in rural areas, where the choice of partners would be expected to be less than in cities, showed higher levels than city dwellers. The prevalence of consanguineous mating in an Israeli-Arab community was found to be

44.3% by Jabar et al (1994), with the highest rates being in rural areas and between first cousins. Amongst the Abbad tribe in Jordan around one third of matings were between first cousins (Nabulsi 1995), and Wahab and Ahmad (1996) recording frequencies of consanguineous mating in rural and urban areas in Swat, Pakistan to be 37.13% and 31.11 % respectively. Similar findings have been reported by AlGazali et al (1997) with respect to al Ain and Dubai cities, United Arab Emirates, and al-Abdulkareem and Ballal (1998) for Damman city Eastern province, Saudi Arabia. These data support Shepher's (1983) contention that there are underlying mechanisms that function to limit incest. Research suggests that except in exceptional circumstances of isolation, consanguineous mating between close relatives will not take place.

Biology and Incest

From the above studies it can be seen readily that even where consanguineous relationships are common, mating with kin closer than first cousin is rare. But it should also be noted that even in cases of first cousin mating negative health consequences are manifested in a variety of forms. Hence, except with respect to those groups where inbreeding has taken place over long periods of time, inbreeding is routinely associated with heavy costs to community health. These costs will be the greatest within those communities where, through lack of opportunities to outbreed due to social or geographic isolation, inbreeding is routinely practised.

From the above discussion the biological context of incest is clear. The closer the genetic relatedness of individuals the greater is the chance that negative health consequences will arise amongst the offspring of any union. Consequently, selective forces would act over time to limit consanguineous mating between close kin. However, where there are few opportunities to mate due to social or geographical isolation, consanguineous mating will be advantageous as the alternative would be to have no offspring. In these circumstances Shepher (1983) has argued that, on genetic grounds, mother-son incest would be the rarest, brother-sister rare but more common, and father-daughter the most common (see above). However, if mating between cousins is available then this would be favoured over closer kin.

In looking at the costs as opposed to the benefits of outbreeding Alexander (1977) revealed that a cost-benefit analysis shows that the balance lies near the level of first cousins in the majority of human societies (see also Shepher 1983). The percentage of genes shared by parents, their offspring and by siblings is 50%, but between first cousins is it only 12.5%, In consequence, statistically there are fewer risks of homozygosity for recessive traits from first cousin mating than with any of the former possible pairings (the rate reducing in line with the reduction in degree of relatedness). This suggests that consanguineous mating between cousins would thus be the most widespread. And the findings cited above do indeed show that first cousin marriages are the most common within inbreeding groups. Hence it would appear to be the case that mechanisms operating within communities to limit or direct the practice of incest do mirror readily understood biological imperatives.

From a Darwinian perspective it would be expected that over time natural selection would lead to the best fit between the advantages and disadvantages of inbreeding and outbreeding being arrived at, and that for the typical community this would be around the level of first cousin mating. This would be the case primevally when smaller populations would have meant fewer opportunity for extended outbreeding, and it has been shown to be the case within contemporary groups where, as with an Amish community in the USA or rural groups in Asia, outbreeding opportunities are limited. In these cases inbreeding practices mirror biological concerns, but it is also known that incest taboos do not mirror exactly expectations of behaviour arising from genetic arguments. In social and cultural terms incest is yet more complex. And to address these aspects of incest, it will be necessary to revisit previous analyses of incest conducted from sociological or anthropological perspectives.

Society, Culture and Incest

There have been a number of reviews of the classic writings on incest provided by anthropologists such as Malinowski and Levi-Strauss. These reviews have provided broad classifications of the various theoretical approaches adopted. Aberle et al (1968), for example, identified six theoretical categories of theory relating to the origin and persistence of the incest taboo: 1) Inbreeding theory , 2) Socialisation theory, 3) Family theory, 4) Theories relating to social and cultural systems, 5) Westermarck's indifference or revulsion theory and finally theories associated with demographic characteristics. Shepher (1983) undertook a similar task and produced an analysis of incest which identified contributions from sociobiology, Freud and the family-socialisation school, and an alliance school. For Shepher, Aberle et al's inbreeding theories and Westermarck's difference theory were subsumed under the heading of sociobiological theory, socialisation theory and family theory under the family-socialisation school, and social, cultural and demographic theories under the alliance school. Meta-analyses of contributions to the study of incest such as these are helpful to the development of new perspectives, but the intention in this current text is not to follow this trend too closely, but instead to provide a novel synthesis that will disclose elements of the structure of incest that have not featured in previous studies. In the following discussion attention will be focused on the nature of the underlying structure of incest that both restricts its practice, and yet simultaneously promotes its continued occurrence.

One common school of thought on incest contends that sexual attraction between members of the same family is a universal characteristic of human nature. The two writers most commonly associated with this view are Freud and Malinowski. The basic position adopted by Freud is that sexual attraction between males and females is always present in all circumstances, even between family members. In consequence, these impulses can only be contained by way of social prohibition. For Freud the first figures of desire for a male child are his mother and sister, and it is only through the construction of restrictions are these impulses contained and eventually redirected. Freud thus not only rejects any notion of there being an aversive reaction arising from adaptive responses to the outcomes of incest, but inverts this causal chain and claims that primary drives are actually directed towards inbreeding. In arguing from this position Freud was then faced with the task of explaining how incest taboos persist universally within human communities, and, in response, he coined the concept of a collective mind within which inhibiting processes dwell and are inherited (Freud 1960). What Freud actually meant by this was that mental processes could be passed on from one generation to another. Indeed in claiming that no one generation would be able wholly to suppress "mental impulses" so that they were eliminated from social and personal life, Freud was clearly referring to a form of genetic inheritance of cognitive states. The reader will be familiar with this concept from the discussion in earlier chapters of the adaptive nature of human instincts, reason and rationality. For Freud, however, these concepts create problems as if it can be accepted that cognitive processes can be inherited then why are inherited feelings of guilt thought to be a more likely source of an incest taboo than an inherited predisposition towards the emergence aversion reactions, as outlined by Westermarck (1894)? Freud fails to provide an adequate account of this inconsistency in his approach. Indeed a convincing explanation of the way in which these conditions came into being is unlikely to be forthcoming. It seems unlikely that the process of natural selection would give rise an outcome whereby a trait is both universal (sexual attraction between males and females in all contexts) and destructive (infused with guilt). As has been discussed in detail above, inbreeding can be a favourable outcome in certain conditions, hence it is improbable that there would be maintained an associated universal guilt. If there was, then social and familial dysfunction would have always arisen from those inbreeding acts that were biologically advantageous as a result of dwelling in conditions of isolation, and this would not have been adaptive.

It is, of course, a contention of Freudian psychoanalysis that psychological dysfunctions do in fact arise within families as a result of this mismatch of sexual attraction and universal guilt. However, this cannot be universal in the way implied by Freud's work as the parallel emergence of these contradictory states would not be adaptive. If inbreeding is sometimes advantageous, then it is adaptive. If sometimes it is not advantageous then the avoidance of inbreeding is also adaptive. Thus incest has what may be termed a contrary adaptiveness, both the execution of the trait and its avoidance are adaptive, but in different circumstances. When outbreeding is available and safe then there is an avoidance of inbreeding, but when outbreeding is unsafe or not available then there is a predisposition towards inbreeding. A predisposition that will vary in amplitude depending upon the nature of the relationship. That is, the sexual behaviour of people towards their kin will be affected by the inbreeding-outbreeding potential of a given environment. Sexual responses will be directed by adaptive cognitive mechanisms that are mapped to the mating context of the external environmental conditions. From an adaptationist perspective no other explanation can clarify the circumstances whereby converse cognitive traits have emerged within human mental life. What Freud observed amongst his clinical population were likely to have been dysfunctions in these mechanisms, rather than the expression of a universal disorder in sexual behaviour.

The concept of a contrary adaptive incest trait will be developed further below, but first attention must be given to the work of Bronislaw Malinowski. In questioning the existence of a universal Oedipus complex, Malinowski was one of the first critics of Freud's theories of sexual development. Malinowski (1960) argued that unlike the competition that exists between father and son in Western patriarchal society, amongst the Melanesian Trobrianders there was no discord emanating in a similar manner. In comparing his findings with those of Freud, Malinowski claimed that whereas from Freud it is claimed that a universal Oedipus complex gives rise to a repressed longing to kill the father, within the matrilineal society of the Triobranders there was otherwise a desire to marry the sister and dispose of the maternal uncle. This comparison of Freud's findings with his own led Malinowski to argue for analyses based on an understanding of the interrelationship between biological influences and social practices. Malinowski agreed with Freud that sexual attraction within the family (or kinship group) is a biological given, but that the expression of this is dependent on forms of social life. The main function of incest taboos was for Malinowski the reduction or elimination of sexual practices that would undermine kinship structure. It was claimed that within societies where incest was allowed stable kinship structures would not form and there would be an absence of social order (Malinowski 1959). However, although Malinowski's work was essentially directed towards a normative sociological analysis where order is seen to be the main function of collective action, he did recognise the complexity of actual practices. He contended that the fixed nature of customs implied by native accounts of incest taboos were in practice modified by what he held to be an underlying human nature (Malinowski 1929). Malinowski's work was thus an important qualification of the work of Freud. Rather than contending that incest taboos arise uniformly across all human societies unchanged, he was able to demonstrate that social contexts have an important impact on actual practices. In this regard his work made an important contribution to our understanding not only of incest, but of the interrelationship that exists between biological predispositions and social forms; between nature and culture.

However, despite the strength of his analysis, one weakness of Malinowski's research on incest was his failure to distinguish between different incestuous dyads within the development of his theoretical perspective. As Shepher (1983) notes, Malinowski fails to explain why Trobrianders react differently to differing forms of incest. Although within Trobriand society brother-sister mating is held to be the worst form of incest, followed by mother-son incest, with father-daughter incest attracting the least negative reaction (though all three are illegal and held to be improper), Malinowski fails to account for these differences in his theoretical reflections. As Shepher (1983) remarks, if incest taboos are about maintaining social order, then social reactions should mirror the degree of threat implied by a given act and, consequently, it might be expected that tension between fathers and sons arising from mother-son incest would be equal to tension arising between mother and daughter as a result of father-daughter incest. As has been noted above, this was not found to be the case. Consequently, although Malinowski's work on incest provided important new insights into this phenomenon, he failed in his attempt to explain the link between biological mechanisms concerned with a supposed universal sexual attraction and sociological functions directed towards the maintenance of social order.

Nevertheless the contribution Malinowski made to the recognition of a variable link between biological mechanisms and social forms, and the disjunction that may arise between social institutions and actual practices is important. This is particularly so with respect to the analysis being presented in this current book, where rather than avoiding or denying inconsistencies in social, cultural or biological processes such emergent characteristics of natural and human systems are placed at the centre of human affairs. Nevertheless, although the interaction between nature and culture which lies at the foundation of social forms such as the incest taboo may not necessarily lead to easily explicable outcomes, through studying such interactions gains can be made in developing a generalised understanding of the processes that underpin the general development of human societies. Incest has proved a fertile area of study in this respect, with the work of Levi-Strauss standing out as a major attempt to uncover the character of certain universal principles that have structured the formation of human culture. Although Freud and Malinowski made significant contributions to an understanding of the interaction between biological processes and social behaviour relating to sexual attraction within kinship groups, it was Levi-Strauss who first sought to show that an incest taboo may be directly associated with the very origin of culture. That is, to argue that incest prohibitions were the raison détre of cultural life.

Levi-Strauss saw incest as being at the intersection of nature and culture. For him, incest was both universal in being part of the natural world, and cultural in that it was subject to institutional control through the operation of norms. The biological aspect of incest taboos gave rise to its universal nature, whilst from culture there stemmed individual differences in particular forms. Levi-Strauss argued that although incest extends beyond the influences of specific historical and geographical boundaries in that it appears throughout human societies, it is nevertheless a fundamental aspect of all cultures. This line of reasoning could have led him to conclude that within biological terms incest avoidance was a cultural expression of the avoidance of inbreeding. However, after considering genetic evidence of the effects of inbreeding on subsequent fitness he discounts such evidence as being the basis of incest taboos, arguing that the regulation of consanguineous marriages would have limited genetic consequences, and that so-called primitive people could not have known of the negative consequences of inbreeding (Levi-Strauss 1969). He took issue with Westermarck's ideas about the existence of a developmental aversive response to family members on the grounds that as incest does exist, and may, he conjectured, be more common than is generally thought to be the case, it is strange to claim that incest gives rise to repugnance. In this regard Levi-Strauss concluded that there would be no point in forbidding that which would rarely take place. He contended that, on the contrary, a society would only forbid that which it brought into being (Levi-Strauss 1969). By which he meant, of course, that if there was an existing aversion to incest there would be no need for laws and norms to prohibit such acts.

One can appreciate why Levi-Strauss could conclude in this manner, however there are other acts which, although they may be abhorrent in most circumstances, are nevertheless both enacted and socially constrained. Murder is one such act. To imply that because something is aversive it will never be undertaken and therefore needs no social constraint is not necessarily the case in all circumstances. What is to be avoided in one setting may be appropriate in another. However, before this line of reasoning is developed further some consideration must be given to the substance of the biological component in his proposed interface between nature and culture.

As has been revealed, the biological component of Levi-Strauss's views on the interface between nature and culture was not an in built aversive reaction to sexual responses to those raised in the same household or family. Instead he argued that nature is transcended through the cultural acquisition of mating rites. Nature gives rise to mating, which is limited by culture to expression in some form of marriage practice. Without culture, alliances are made simply by way of mating, but through culture this becomes socially endorsed and transformed into marriage. The cultural form of mating is marriage and thus mating alliances become cultural property rather than solely an outcome of a biological act. Once this transition had taken place then the control and regulation of marriage enabled gains to be made in forging alliances with those outside the kinship group. Levi-Strauss contended that as in many traditional societies marriages are an economic arrangement, it follows that given inequalities in resources, some women (those in possession of greater than average resources) could be considered to be a scarce asset. Such women, he argued, could function in the creation of new alliances. To achieve this men were willing to forgo their access to female kin so that the gains to be made from marrying them out could be achieved. In this sense Levi-Strauss claimed that broader societies extending beyond narrow kinship groups stemmed from the control and revocation of sexual contact with close kin. From this developed wider social units.

Levi-Strauss's analysis of incest fits within what is generally known as the Alliance School, from which it is argued that incest prohibitions arise from a will to link the nuclear family to wider social units and thus forge political and economic alliances (Shepher 1983). The Alliance School has been criticised because it fails to examine closely differences between incest rules and rules relating to exogamy (Shepher 1983). As Schneider noted in an unpublished 1956 paper cited in Shepher 1983, alliance theory cannot account for mother-son prohibitions in patrilineal systems and father-daughter prohibitions in matrilineal systems, in addition to other cases of mismatch between rules governing marriage and prohibitions on incest. Later, Schneider contended that incest prohibitions are much more than breeding regulations and that such regulations are not directly related to a general tendency amongst people to avoid sexual contact with members of their primary socialisation group (Scheider 1976). In making this comment Scheider indicated that inbreeding avoidance may indeed be grounded biologically, but of greater importance in terms of offering a critique of Levi-Stauss is his repudiation of the key component of the alliance school, that inbreeding avoidance is linked to incest prohibitions relating to the cultural objective of forming alliances with those outwith the family or socialisation unit. As he and others have pointed out, many writers, including Levi-Strauss, have at times conflated marriage and sexual relationships. Incest prohibitions are as often founded on marital status as on consanguinity. For example, Fortes (1949) described a bilateral classificatory system for the Tallensi, W. Africa in which sexual relations with a sister or daughter is held to be disreputable, whilst that with the wife of a father, brother or son was viewed with great censure. Thus although sexual relationships with female consanguines could be permitted within tribal institutions, that with the wife of someone from the same lineage was considered a great wrong. In contrast, Rattray's (1929) analysis of incest amongst the Ashanti, W. Africa showed the opposite classification. Consanguineous incest carried a sentence of death, whilst sexual relations with the wife of another attracted only an adultery payment. Other cases could be cited that also show the importance of marital status as well as consanguinity to previous definitions of incest. For example, Goody (1968) reported that the LoDagaa, W. Africa had a classificatory system similar to the Tallensi. However, the main conclusion that can be derived from these examples is that a great deal of previous work has been centred on analyses of indigenous interpretations of rules about sexual relationships, and has paid little or only secondary attention to consanguineous relations in practice. If attention is focused more narrowly on the issue of consanguinity rather than social relatedness then it can be seen that even though a particular social group may have as a higher order category of offence relationships outwith the consanguineous group, this does not mean that relations between siblings or parents and offspring is normative. Indeed Fortes (1949) recorded that although amongst the Tallensi sibling incest was not classified as highly as adultery in terms of the degree of offence, it nevertheless seldom occurred and was not thought to be an expected or desired outcome. Fortes recorded a discussion with an informant who revealed that sexual desires for a sister would not occur from the circumstances of familiarity that existed between brother and sister (Fortes 1949). Thus the main theoretical flaw in the work of those who have concentrated on incest and relationships external to the family has been to ignore activities such as sibling incest. There is little evidence that these frequently occur even when they are not formally proscribed. This is somewhat ironic as critics of biological-based incest theories such as Levi-Strauss and Freud argued that it would not be necessary to proscribed something that did not take place, and yet with the Tallensi there is clear evidence that this situation did in fact arise. There are proscriptions on sexual relations other than with consanguines but not for those between brother and sister, between whom sexual relations do not take place as a norm. This suggests that the prohibitions are directed elsewhere than upon inbreeding with close kin, which is limited generally by mechanisms other than those of a social or cultural nature.

What social science in general has brought to the understanding of incest is a sociological and cultural perspective that has illustrated that prohibitions around sexual relations are complex and variable between different social groups. Within some communities inbreeding between close kin is prohibited and can carry a penalty of death, whilst in others there may be no such rules or punishments. However, as revealed by Fortes with respect to the Tallensi, this does not mean that such acts are a routine part of kinship relationships. Often sexual relations that are outwith rules and prohibitions have not been commented on in the same way. For example, Shepher notes that Goody's research (1956) implies that within a matrilineal society a father could have sexual relations with his unmarried daughter, and that in a patrilineal society a son with his unmarried mother, whereas in fact no evidence of these sexual relations taking place was found. As Murdock (1949) noted from a review of anthropological data that cites the intensity of taboos on sexual relations, these are always stronger with respect to consanguineous kin than classificatory kin (though intensity varies between different societies). And evidence from other sources suggests that it is universally the case that incest between close kin is not commonplace, even when there is an absence of direct prohibitions. In the findings cited above on the outcomes of inbreeding within various societies, first cousin mating comprised the vast majority of cases considered, those with closer kin are very rare.

Overall it appears from the evidence that notwithstanding the complexity of sexual taboos between different social groups, restrictions of either a formal or informal manner exist with respect to sexual relations between close kin. By informal is meant that in the absence of rules and regulations there is nevertheless a value system in existence within which consanguineous relations are either proscribed or otherwise undesired and unexpected, as with the Tallensi. What this means is that a mechanism other than one based on formal institutions, rules and prohibitions must, therefore, be in operation for those groups within which formal restrictions do not exist. And if this is the case then there would be a need to examine whether or not it is likely that such a mechanism operates universally. This preliminary conclusion returns us to the work of Westermarck, who, as will be remembered from the brief introduction to his work above, argued that there exists sexual indifference or revulsion to members of the same socialising group; that is, those who shared the same childhood environment.

Westermarck and the Biosocial Perspective on Incest

The central concern within Westermarck's work was with sexual intercourse between close kin. Unlike many anthropologists of his time and later, Westermarck (1894) argued that incest regulations could not be derived from rules relating to exogamy. For Westermarck incest did not occur between mother and son, father and daughter or brother and sister because of proscriptions, but because of an avoidance instinct which made such unions an impossibility. (It should be noted that although it is now known widely that sexual abuse does occur within some families, this was not an aspect of Westermarck's work. His research was directed towards unfolding the foundations of normative action within communities.) His reasoning in this regard was informed by the belief that inbreeding would over time be detrimental to the species, and thus in consequence, through the process of natural selection, such acts would be attenuated. Given that Westermarck wrote before Mendel's work on the mechanisms of genetic inheritance became known in Western Europe his insights were in advance of his time, and led to many attacks on his work. However, although as a Darwinian Westermarck believed that the family unit formed, by way of natural selection, within the context of the extended length of dependency of human children (they are cared for up to and even beyond the age of sexual maturity), he did not contend that his proposed innate aversion to incest was directed specifically towards consanguines. He held that an instinct could not discern between kin and others (Westermarck 1891). To support this argument he cited evidence of incest that had taken place between close kin who had been separated during childhood and then reunited. He contended that it was not consanguinity per se that gave rise to an aversive reaction to sexual contact, but having lived closely together during childhood.

Working within the paradigm developed by Westermarck, Shepher carried out research on sexual relations between members of kibbutzim during the 1970s. His data showed that of 42 second generation adults in the "Ya'ara" community there not a single case of erotic behaviour took place between children raised in the same educational group, and there was only one case of sexual activity between second generation individuals raised in separate peer groups (Shepher 1983). However, when male and female children were not born into a peer group but joined it later, Shepher reports that sexual attraction to other group members was high and preferred over other relationships. Marriage followed the same pattern, in that no-one married within their peer group. Shepher (1971) also undertook a survey of 2769 married couples from 211 different kibbutzim, and found not one case where the married couple had been socialised together without interruption. And these findings arose even though there was no taboo against such marriages, or against sexual play between kibbutzim.

This is strong evidence in favour of Westermarck' theory of innate aversion based upon a shared socialising environment. Further evidence is provided by Shepher's (1983) review of the work of Wolf in the late 1960s and 1970, and Wolf and Huang in the 1970s on the Hokkien-speaking people of Hsiachichou in northern Taiwan. Wolf identified three forms of marriage amongst this group of people; a patrilocal type, an uxorilocal and sim-pua types. In the first two types of marriage the couple first meet as adults, but in the latter type the future bride is adopted by the family of the intended bridegroom. The adopted girl is raised within the family alongside the boy. When the two children reach adulthood they are married by the head of the family through a subdued ceremony in which they are informed that they are from that point on husband and wife. Wolf reports that these latter couples are highly reluctant to marry. After considering possible reasons for such reluctance based on the lack of status of the ceremony or the absence of social or economic significance in terms of constructing new alliances between different families, Wolf concludes that the reluctance is based upon a lack of sexual attraction between the couple. In support of this argument Wolf (1970) demonstrated that the frequency of extramarital relations was higher amongst couples from sim-pua marriages than the other two common types, particularly with respect to married women. Wolf reported that within northern Taiwan 33% of women from sim-pua marriages committed adultery, whereas only 11% from other marriages did so. Wolf's explanation for the lack of sexual attraction is based ideas concerned with the repression of "strong impulses" directed towards the family motivated by a fear of punishment (Wolf 1966). Shepher (1983) was not convinced by Wolf's interpretation of his data, and argued that the absence of reporting on the ages of specific couples in the study meant that consideration of the effect of co-socialisation could not be undertaken. Shepher (1983) concludes his review of Wolf's work by stating that in his view those cases cited by Wolf are those where the couple were co-socialised during early childhood and were thus negatively imprinted with respect to mutual sexual activity. In support of this view he points out that although within several native Australian cultures prospective wives are also reared in the intended husbands family problems of sexual aversion do not arise (as would be expected from Wolf's interpretation of his data). Shepher notes that this may be explained by the age difference between the couple when adoption took place. He makes the assumption that the age difference was great enough that negative imprinting during early socialisation did not take place. Hence, he argues, taken together research on relationships formed in kibbutzim and through sim-pua marriages provide support for Westermarck innate avoidance of incest with respect to sexual relations between siblings. With these ideas to hand it is now possible to consider what part adaptation may play in the avoidance of incest.

Adaptation and Incest Avoidance

Throughout this chapter a considerable amount of evidence has been presented concerning the biological and cultural components of incest taboos. Shepher's work has revealed that in adaptive terms incest can be beneficial in circumstances of extreme isolation, but when outbreeding is associated with fewer risks than inbreeding it will be preferred biologically. In this regard there can be said to have evolved the possibility that natural selection led to a situation whereby within social groups inbreeding is balanced between risks associated with inbreeding and outbreeding, and that this would vary between groups depending on the environmental circumstances. However, as Shepher argued with respect to sibling incest, inbreeding would only be preferred if the costs of outbreeding were 1.5 times greater. That is, inbreeding would only be favoured if there existed a 66% chance that death would result from attempts to outbreed (Shepher 1983). Hence a mechanism which calculates the balance between these two possible forms of action will, it is argued, have arisen adaptively. Westermarck considered this mechanism to be grounded in an innate aversion towards those present in the same household during early development, but from Shepher's work it can now be postulated that although some form of aversion may be the basis of incest avoidance the circumstances within which this operates will vary. When outbreeding is associated with severe negative consequences then inbreeding will, from the above analysis, take place. Consequently any innate aversive reaction to inbreeding must be moderated by external circumstances. An innate aversion would therefore only operate when outbreeding does not carry related high risks. This means that incest avoidance is a dynamic component of human nature, rather than either being present or absent. Environmental circumstances will have a great impact upon the profile of sexual relations in a specific group. If this is so, and the evidence presented suggests that this may indeed be the case, then the underlying mechanism of incest avoidance must comprise a cognition component. The monitoring of the environment required to assess or otherwise arrive at a stance with respect to the balance of costs for inbreeding and outbreeding could only be achieved cognitively. Even if the eventual trigger that elicited a sexual response was, say, hormonal, the calculation of costs and benefits could only take place as part of the ongoing appraisal of the environment by certain of the perceptual and cognitive processes comprising the human mind. These would be adaptive components arising from the process of natural selection.

The nature of possible mechanisms for the operation of an innate aversion may be suggested by the work of Cosmides cited above. As you will recall from chapter three, it has been argued from research in evolutionary psychology that important aspects of human cognition are adaptive, derived from the circumstances of a primeval life through natural selection. Such adaptive components of cognition have been termed Darwinian algorithms, and it was suggested above that these may form the basis of emergent cognitive modules. It seems more than reasonable to suppose that the mechanism underlying the delimitation of sexual relations would to some degree resemble a Darwinian algorithm in form and function, and that such an algorithm(s) could underpin a module associated with sexual behaviour. However, unlike that associated with a "look for cheaters strategy", an algorithm functioning in regard to inbreeding would be either overtly dynamic in that predispositions to sexual relations would change according to environmental variations, or it would be dispersed differentially throughout a given population. Shepher's idea that an innate aversion would be like a once occurring imprinting event seems less likely than the alternative as there would then be no future possibility of change in the nature of sexual relations should environmental circumstances change and a group that previously experienced opportunities to outbreed became isolated. In fact the possibility of there being a dynamic component to a possible incest algorithm as part of a broader cognitive module related to sexual behaviour is suggested by Shepher's analysis of differences in cost for differing inbreeding events. As discussed above, his analysis shows that in genetic terms, mother-son incest would be the rarest form of inbreeding, brother-sister more common, and father-daughter the most common when cousins are unavailable. Otherwise mating between cousins would be favoured over closer kin. Hence orientations towards kin as possible mates is differential. Any biologically-based trigger mechanism for incest avoidance is thus discriminatory between differing consanguines. This suggest strongly that there is no simple on/off trigger based on an imprinting event between consanguines. In any event, Shepher's empirical work is limited to generalisations about siblings, and says nothing about parent-child relationships. If each of these qualifications are considered, then it becomes clear that imprinting as such is unlikely to be the primary basis for biologically founded incest avoidance. From present knowledge about the role of natural selection in the formation of certain cognitive processes, it appears that some form of Darwinian algorithm is the most likely basis of any aversive reaction.

If, as the evidence suggests, this is so, then how is this algorithm likely to operate? By once again adopting an adaptationist perspective it seems likely that in conditions of social isolation almost everybody is capable of engaging in sexual relations with close kin. If the alternative was true, that the potential for inbreeding was dispersed throughout a given population, then it would be expected that those incapable of inbreeding would have reduced fitness and would thus have been eliminated from the gene pool. Although it could be argued that a potential for inbreeding could be maintained within a population as a recessive trait, it is unlikely that heterozygosity for the trait would be maintained. When the primeval population of early humankind was very low it is likely that groups were very often relatively isolated, hence those individuals that were unable to inbreed as a consequence of the maintenance of their innate aversion would quickly disappear from the population and, in consequence, homozygosity for the trait would be rapidly established. A potential to inbreed would be a primary trait, those without it could not produce progeny and their genotype would thus not contribute further to the genetic future of the group.

The actual mechanism through which any Darwinian algorithm could be expressed must at this time be the subject only of broad speculation. However, from what is known about the role of pheromones in stimulating sexual activity it may be that such sex hormones play some part in triggering cognitive action, but visual clues too may play an important part in the elicitation of a sexual response. Whatever the actual range and operation of such signals may be, and we may never know, it seems more than mere speculation to suggest that familiarity is a key to reduced sexual response and a stimulus to search for outbreeding opportunities. The continuous presence of close kin may thus lead to a reduction in sexual attractiveness, rather than elicit a permanent aversive reaction. Nevertheless, this is not to suggest that the process of inhibition is solely a mechanical response to olfactory or visual stimuli. Given that there are always going to be risks of some magnitude associated with outbreeding, and given the intricacy of the socialised intelligence of the human mind that features both self-conscious awareness and subconscious processing, it is unlikely that the mechanism would be based solely on a stimulus-response mechanism. The likelihood is that complex forecasts of the outcome of future actions will be derived cognitively. The benefit accruing to individuals as a result of particular actions will be a part of such forecasting or cognitive appraisal. If this is so, then as with other cognitive functions described above, it can be expected that there will be some variation in response between individuals. Notwithstanding any species constraints on inbreeding potential, if inbreeding is subject to the operation of Darwinian algorithms grounded biologically in networks of neural tissue, then there will be variability in operation due to the stochastic processes of brain development which give rise to differences in brain structure even between identical twins, and also through differences in experience that effect subsequence neural developments, as discussed in chapter two.

In this regard patterns of inbreeding responses are both universal and particular. It is being argued that the potential to inbreed is widespread through humankind, but constrained within contexts relating to the existence or otherwise of conditions of social isolation. The substance of inbreeding is universal, but given that it is grounded both cognitively and biologically, it is variable between individuals. Any particular state is a emergent outcome of the interconnectiveness that will exist between cognitive and environmental conditions. There will be constraints on inbreeding responses that will emerge cognitively by way of specific environmental conditions and structure sexual responses. In consequence, each individual's disposition towards sexual activity will be unique, arising both genetically and through developmental processes. Behaviour, though, will be structured through social norms and institutions governing sexual acts and will thus appear largely uniform.

If this is so, then it is legitimate to ask why rules about incest are so variable between different cultures? The biological view would be that only incest between kin more closely related than cousins should be proscribed. But, as is known from the ethnographic record this is not the case. In general this is a problem of definition. It was stated above that in many cases when anthropologists have been writing about incest they have in fact been commenting on marriage proscriptions. And, although similarities do exist, say as between the Nuer and Western society as commented on by Goody (1968), there is also great variability. What seems to be happening is that deep-seated rules about inbreeding and outbreeding, grounded in adaptive responses to reproductive outcomes associated with genetic fitness, find different expression at the level of sociality and culture. The cognitive mechanisms that underpin sexual behaviour find different form under differing environmental conditions. Diversity of outcomes between one culture an another stem from this differential expression of a universal avoidance mechanism associated with inbreeding. The fact that such a mechanism is a universal aspect of human agency means that there will always be rules about sexual behaviour between relatives, but the form that these take will depend upon the social and cultural environment within which they are expressed. The dissimilarities in the character of incest taboos that exist from one culture to the next can thus be seen to stem from the differential modified expansion of a universal cognitive monitoring of inbreeding behaviour. The great diversity of incest taboos can thus be seen to derive from biosocial mechanisms rather than being the phenomenological outcome of subjective cultural practices. Specific practices are thus an emergent outcome of biological, cognitve and cultural processes.

This view leads readily to a critique of postmodern social science. In the next chapter it will be argued that a synthesis of Darwinian evolutionary theory and complexity theory can underscore a new approach to social theory that avoids the weaknesses of both modern and postmodern social science, whilst at the same time maintaining their respective interests in the uncovering of objective causal mechanisms and the exploration of cultural and social diversity, contingency and unpredictability. Chapter six will argue for the adaptive and complex foundations of an emerging nonmodern social theory.

6 Nonlinearity in the Social World

The discussion of the cognitive and cultural evolution of humankind contained within the previous chapters has drawn attention to the way novel insights into this developmental process can be gained from utilising ideas from complexity theory and theories of human evolution. The essential core of this emerging analysis is that certain components of cognition and cultural life can be understood as being the expression of an underlying causative agency, that has arisen by way of selective processes, within a complex, multidimensional and interconnected material world.

A simple example may make this statement somewhat clearer. All rabbits in the UK are burrowing animals. Each possesses an algorithm that directs the animal to to dig a burrow as a secure form of accommodation (but not, of course, absolutely protective against all predators). This burrow making behaviour is a species level condition that determines an important aspect of the material life of the rabbit. Every time one sees rabbits in the wild, it would be possible to trace them back to a warren of tunnels. However, although all rabbits belong to a burrow, all burrows are different. Once the algorithm for building a burrow is expressed, it then unfolds within the context of constraints within the material world. Sometimes the ground may be soft and deep, other times shallow and hard, sometimes within a wood with an extensive network of roots and yet others in the open by the side of a ploughed field. To a large extent, each time a rabbit or community of rabbits begins to construct a warren they will encounter a unique set of circumstances, different from those encountered by any other rabbit community. In the same way, although all web building spiders have webs, the webs of the same species of spider are always different from each other. A warren, or a spiders web (or an ants nest or other construction produce by animal life forms) will vary to some extent from any other construction of the same type as a product of the prevailing material conditions. In this way the same underlying causal agent, such as a mental algorithm, can give rise to infinite variability in the actual form an outcome takes within the material world. This variability stems from the interaction between the behavioural expression of the algorithm and prevailing material conditions. In this sense the warren or web that arises can be said to be an emergent outcome of all the interactions taking place between the interconnected elements that comprise the warren or web building scenario.

This is the central premise underlying the discussion in chapter five. Species level restrictions on the occurrence of inbreeding and outbreeding give rise to incest taboos at the cultural level that will vary from one culture to another as a reflection of differing material conditions. That is, incest taboos are emergent. This is not to suggest that there is a direct relationship between given material conditions and incest taboos, this would be to depict a simple causal mechanism divorced from other aspects of human material and cultural life. What is being suggested is that certain material conditions (such as those that give rise to nomadic behaviour) may lead to cultural practices that engender particular family structures, and that in turn these may give rise to marriage conventions that lead to rules about inbreeding and outbreeding being expressed in ways particular to the unique nature of a given community. A given taboo is thus seen as an emergent outcome of the interconnectiveness that exists between embodied aspects of human agency, existing cultural practices and material conditions. This means that to argue that an aspect of human agency or a cultural practice is determine by underlying causal processes, it does not mean that outcomes can be known with certainty. As what takes place historically is seen as the emergent outcome of constantly changing sets of relationships, outcomes cannot be predicted in any exact way.

The implication of this relationship between deep-lying causal structures (that have arisen as embodied aspects of human agency by way of natural selection) and the emergence of cultural outcomes within the material world is that cultural life, at least in part, contains elements of unpredictability. That is, the resolution of underlying causal structures and material conditions at a given moment gives rise to emergent phenomena the exact character of which cannot not be known prior to their appearance as specific outcomes. This being the case, then not only is it not possible to predict the form that cultural phenomena will take, but the prediction of change will also be problematic. The material and cultural worlds exist in a dialectical relationship between the way the material world constrains the cultural expression of causative structures, and cultural practices transform the material world. Or, rather, outcomes for humankind are an emergent consequence of the interconnectivity that exists between all aspects of human agency, both embodied and cultural, and nature.

In consequence of the way in which species level constraints, the cultural world and materiality are interwoven the world of human affairs contains a core of unpredictability. This means that early post-Enlightenment attempts to construct a predictive science of human life that could lead to a systematic and ordered society were based upon false assumptions about human nature and cultural change. Such attempts failed because they were grounded on false propositions about human nature, the epistemological status of culture and the interconnectiveness that exists between human agency and materiality. In seeking to control nature and forge a utopian state, modern social theory failed to uncover the way in which humankind is realised moment by moment from the interweaving of nature and culture.

Unachieved Modernity

The central theme that informs modernity is a belief that through the application of science and technology humankind can progress towards a perfected state within which all social problems will have been surmounted. The modern perspective held that there would come a time when a new science of the social would lead to the achievement of a rational social order through the removal of disorder and uncertainty. A perfected social order would prevail, within which harmony would be the norm and deviance eliminated. This post-Enlightenment period in the development of social theory was characterised by a general belief that science and technology could solve all social problems. As Bauman (1991) noted, although based on atrocities of a horrific type and magnitude the actions of Hitler and Stalin, were in many respects a logical outcome of the post-Enlightenment period, based as the were on the belief that societies can be moulded according to scientific principles into a utopian state. Through reasoning, it was held, the perfect state could be designed and accomplished. The authors of modern social science, and those that sought through political means to apply such reasoning to the management of human affairs, falsely assumed that their endeavours could mirror the ordering of nature reflected in the natural sciences. The founding of modern social science was based on a desire to realise within social science the kind of systematic knowledge associated with the natural sciences.

Through the application of a formal and systematic rationality the intention was to transcend disorder in social affairs. Within modern social theory explanations of human agency were founded upon an unfolding of ordered universal conditions of human existence.

Comte's sociology, Marx's theory of historical materialism and Levi Strauss's anthropology of the structure of myths are all examples of attempts to produce a systematic account of deep-lying ordered structures beneath human agency. And all these attempts had in common a belief that order rather than contingency underpins human life. But, as history has revealed, such attempts were found to be limited. In separating order from disorder, nature from culture, such accounts could not hold pace with the changing nature of human affairs. The desire to found a predictive science of society was unfulfilled.

History has recorded that the attempts of Hilter, Stalin and other post-Enlightenment attempts at social engineering were unsuccessful. The external world turned out to be more difficult to manipulate than had been anticipated. And, in addition, people were found to respond unpredictably to attempts to structure their daily existence according to formal and centralised control of economic and other activity. The recent failure of the Eastern European centralised socialist economies is one clear example of the difficulties encountered when seeking to determine human action according to a scientific plan. A problem perhaps first articulated by C. Wright Mills who commented in the late 1950s on the inability of humankind to comprehend the totality of their rational social, industrial and economic constructions. For Mills (1959) the promise of the Enlightenment was lost when the rules and procedures of the modern world extended beyond the ability of people to comprehend their nature. At this point, it could be argued, humankind became alienated from their own constructions and the Enlightenment project failed. In this sense the promise of the modern project within social science was never realised. Attempts to order society stalled and remained an unachieved ambition of largely 19th scientists, social scientists and philosophers. The endeavour within the modern project to construct a systematic and predictive social science that could lead to the founding of an ordered society failed because no account was made of the contingent character of human life. Rather than living a perpetually ordered existence, life is often unpredictable and irregular. And the foundations of this unpredictability exist at every moment of the realisation of the individual, society and culture.

There are three key causes of the immanent unpredictability and irregularity. Firstly, humankind was an emergent property of nature. Humankind emerged by way of natural selection acting within a complex highly interconnected natural system of living organisms. Secondly, a cultural life arose as an emergent outcome of an interweaving between an adaptive symbolic reasoning and a complex social life; this latter itself a species level condition of early humans. Thirdly, from the beginning the emergence of culture (as the material and cognitive representation of a collective symbolic order) always took place within the context of certain constraints within the natural world. Culture is always in part a representation of humankind's location in nature; both in a contemporary sense and from an evolutionary perspective. Every time we eat, have sex, talk (gossip), meet new people and communicate these events in whatever way we choose they are always recapitulations of aspects of our evolutionary past and outcomes of our enduring embeddedness in the natural world. The modern project thus failed because it did not take account of these fundamental aspects of human existence, the character of which suggest contingency, variability, unpredictability and nonlinearity. Modern social science seeks to make predictions from within an ordered view of social life, whereas the evidence seems to suggest a universe of great interconnectivity where outcomes are the result of chance configurations rather than by way of systematic regularities.

We Have Never Been Modern

The title of this section has been taken from the English language edition of a book by Bruno Latour first published in 1991 as *Nous n'avons jamias été modernes*. Latour's thesis is that the claim of modernity that nature and society are separate is based upon false assumptions. Rather than science having become a practice purified of cultural influences, he argues that everywhere scientific projects are infused with cultural moments. At the beginning of the above text Latour makes reference to the contents of his daily newspaper. He notes that there are articles detailing measurements taken of the ozone layer above the Antarctic, changes in manufacturing processes to eliminate chlorofluorocarbons, heads of state involved with issues of chemistry, aerosols and inert gases, arguments between meteorologist and chemists, and debates between politicians and ecologists and international treaties and the rights of future generations. Throughout the paper, comments Latour, the most esoteric sciences are intermingled with politics. A discussion of the AIDS virus spans sex, the unconscious, Africa, tissue cultures, DNA and San Francisco. The paper, though, still employed headings such as Economy, Politics, Science, Books, Culture, Religion and Local Events as though none of the above had appeared (Latour 1993). Latour's point was that the evidence of a daily paper, given by way of the form ideas were presented, illustrated the inseparability of scientific discourses on nature and cultural interests expressed within political actions. For Latour the AIDS virus was not solely a natural phenomenon, but in terms of its position with regard to humankind, it was also, in part, cultural. For Latour social analysts have cut the Gordian knot and placed on one side the knowledge of things, and on the other power and human politics. Instead of seeking to discover the way nature and culture are interwoven, Latour states that the routine approach to analysis is to segment nature-culture events into either nature, politics or discourse. Latour's solution, though, is to avoid the separating out of nature from culture and instead translate the networks of interconnections that he terms Ariadne's thread of interwoven stories.

Latour does not reject modern scientific thinking, but rather seeks to modify its scope so that the total separation of humans and nonhumans is put aside. He presents an analysis that claims that the modern project is based upon a constitution comprising three guarantees. The first is that although humans construct nature, nature is as if humans did not construct it. The second guarantee claims that although humans do not construct society, society is as if it is so constructed. And, thirdly, nature and society must remain absolutely distinct, and purification (the creation of human and nonhuman elements) must be kept distinct from mediation (the construction of hybrids comprising both nature and culture). Through citing the work of Boyle and Hobbs, Latour reveals that from their analyses it is possible for the moderns to claim concurrently that both nature and culture are the product of human agency, and yet infinitely transcendent. In this way the modern constitution, so defined by Latour, asserts the total separation of humans and nonhumans, and yet simultaneously cancels out such separation (Latour 1993). It is this aspect of modernity that Latour seeks to refute in reclaiming an inseparability of nature and culture. For Latour the world is infused with hybrids; with mediation or translation between human and nonhuman elements. In this sense the world has never been modern, but is rather nonmodern in that the separation claimed from the Enlightenment onwards has never been sustainable.

In this regard this present analysis agrees with that of Latour. The human world is an interwoven fabric comprising an inseparable nature-culture matrix. But beyond this the two analyses diverge. Latour claims that his notion of translation or network (or mediation) is more subtle than the concept of system, more historical than formulations of structure and more empirical than ideas about complexity (Latour 1993). This is the most surprising turn in his analysis as because everywhere throughout the text there are phrases that appear primarily to be a grounded re-writing of some of the main tenets of complexity theory; of studies of dynamical systems that, depending on certain conditions, comprise both ordered and chaotic states. Indeed the ways Latour describes the characteristics of his nonmodern world resonate clearly with descriptions of certain features of complex.

Latour wants to reclaim the middle ground between nature and culture. The space within which nature and culture infinitely bind together to produce endless hybrids. The ordered world of modernity within which nature and culture are separated is, within Latour's analysis, seen to be a fiction, a product of attempts towards the establishment of an political epistemology founded on a cleaving of the natural and social worlds. But the resultant perception of the possibility of this ordered state is immediately challenged as quasi-objects, neither wholly of nature or culture) shuffle dissimilar periods, ontologies and genres (Latour 1993). As a result history is not seen to flow continuously from period to period, but instead appears as a mosaic or hotchpotch of mismatched events difficult to unravel in any consistent manner. Rather than there being a laminar flow of history, there is otherwise a turbulent rush of rapids and eddies (Latour 1993). Latour also describes boundary events that exist between order and chaos, as defined by Kauffman (1993). He records that nature and society can be compared to the movement of continents defined by plate tectonics. Those who want to understand the relationship between nature and culture must do as the geologist does when they wish to understand the formation of mountains by way of continental drift (though he does not specifically make this last point, the rhetoric employed does appear to indicate this interest), they must observe, "go down to", the "searing rifts" [where there are new beginnings] and approach the "mixing" that will become aspects of nature or the social (Latour 1993: 87). Latour wants to reassert the importance of the indivisibility of nature and culture in the formation of human events. He wants to regain what he terms the "Middle Kingdom" where nature does to revolve around culture, nor culture around nature, but both around a collective from which both emerge. Nature and culture are the satellites of the Middle Kingdom (Latour 1993: 79).

A close reading of Latour's book will reveal that beneath the rhetorical turns of phrase is an analysis that fits closely with contemporary applications of complexity theory to the social sciences. The references to hybrids, turbulence, nonlaminar flow, boundary events between order and chaos indicate clearly an appreciation of characteristics of nonlinear systems. Indeed there seems to be a strong trend within postmodern writing to draw on insights that closely match fundamental characteristics of complex systems and chaotic behaviour. That is systems of very large dimensions, sensitively dependent upon initial conditions that exhibit emergent properties. Another way of saying the same as Latour is to describe the human world as being from moment to moment an emergent property of a complex system comprising a very large number of material and cultural elements. Hybrids are moments of emergence within this complex system. Events will sometimes be ordered but they may also be chaotic. The evolution or progress of such systems follows the trajectory of a strange attractor, and thus lies between ordered and chaotic states. The modern project failed not because of the failure of a mystical Constitution (perhaps a reified concept?), but because the human world can be highly unpredictable. Linear attempts to grasp the nature of human existence are grounded on a false conception of the human world. Social engineering, perhaps the corner stone of the modern project, can progress but poorly in such turbulent systems as appear to define both the cultural and natural world. In this Latour's analysis fits well with the preceding discussion in this chapter on the failings of modern social theory. Nevertheless, notwithstanding agreements between the two analyses with respect to the broad direction of the central critique of modern social science contained in both works, postmodern approaches also contain analytic weaknesses. It follows from this that a critique of aspects of postmodern thinking must follow that of the modern project.

Latour is not alone in his attempts to describe the complex nature of the human world by way of postmodern rhetoric. This is a consistent feature of postmodern social science in general. However, Latour has an optimistic strand to his work, seeking as he does to move beyond the nihilism of most postmodern writing, the unattainability of modernity and the unproductive premodern thesis grounded on mystical beliefs about nature and culture. Nevertheless, his attempts to forge a new perspective on the relationship between nature and culture is still obscured by the individuality of his writing, a trend common within the postmodern school. Often contemporary social theorists engulf their insights into the unpredictable nature of the human world in terms that lead to a reduction in clarity rather than increased accessibility. A point made well by Sokal and Bricmont (1997) in their rigorous critique of some of Frances best known postmodern thinkers. Postmodern writing often confuses rather than illuminates. But problems with the postmodern perspective are not limited to matters of style. In offering a critique of modernity by way of uncovering the existence of immanent contingency and irregularity, postmodern writing has forsworn any attempt to uncover objective or universal characteristics of nature, culture and human agency. In side-stepping one problem they have created another. Hence the postmodern perspective too requires a critique if some objective ground is to be regained.

Complexity and Postmodernity

Attempts to construct a society of order failed because change within social and cultural contexts was irregular and unpredictable. Although the modern project brought great increases in technology and wealth, it did not bring forth a rational and ordered society as anticipated by early post-Enlightenment classical social theorists such as Comte and Durkheim. As discussed above, the failure of the modern project was, and continues to be, recognised by a group of social scientists and historians whose work comprises the what has become to be known as the postmodern framework. A complete description of current postmodern approaches within the social sciences would require far more space than is available here as postmodernism has many different forms. Loosely, though, the emergence of postmodern social theory stemmed from a perceived need to address critically of the problems and limitations of modernity. It is a perspective, particularly in poststructuralists forms (as represented for example in the work of Baudrillard, Foucault, Lacan and others), that argues that all human knowledge is infused with personal aims and cultural perspectives that arise within particular historical contexts. It is thus a central feature within poststructuralist discourses that all theory is problematic as there can be no basis for an appeal to a reality independent of the meanings and knowledge that underpin specific cultures. No particular analysis of either the cultural or natural world is held to be either preeminent or enduring. For poststructuralist there can be no access to an objective truth as all theory is a historical product of the dialectical relationship between the subject and discursive practices. And even in this regard, especially within Foucauldian analysis, the subject is subordinated to discourse. The subject is seen merely as an arbitrary occupier of an historically given discursive space. Thus reasoning and identity are held to be solely an outcome of prevalent discursive practices.

In offering a critique of modernity and the failed attempt to derive a predictive science of social and cultural life, the postmodern movement has usefully drawn attention to the enduring irregularities, uncertainties, disparities of social and cultural life. The inability of the modern project to deal with uncertain social and cultural outcomes and identify a universal order that underpins cultural and social phenomena has been the starting point for a reinterpretation of social and cultural life based upon an acceptance of unpredictability, diversity and irregularity. Rather than being ordered, human life became to be seen as being a contingent outcome, that existence lacks certainty (Bauman 1991).

For many, this development within social theory provided a perspective that facilitated the re-positioning of previously dominant perspectives. In consequence narratives previously situated outwith the dominant narratives of a given epoch could be granted a new and equal status. In the place of constructions that viewed the world by way of single mode of reasoning, there has instead been patterned a plurality of discourses through which have been constructed a plethora of analytic paradigms and forms of knowledge. In many respects this has been emancipatory in that new perspectives on the human condition have been enabled and perspectives on gender such as those featured in feminist and masculinist writing, as well as new work on sexuality and sexual identity developed.

In this regard the postmodern movement has been a fruitful source of new insights and has engendered a range of important and previously unexplored orientations to lasting questions about human agency and identity. But postmodern social science has also, at least in part, nihilistic consequences. In constituting knowledge as being the outcome of an historical dialectic between the subject and culture, the possibility of developing universal theories on humankind are ruled out. And, in addition, in consequence of the central position on the subject that characterises sociology and social anthropology, that the subject is both the source and object of knowledge, an understanding of human agency is developed that is devoid nature. In separating out the subject from nature, both sociology and social anthropology remove the possibility of uncovering the subject except as a contingent property of cultural forms. In denying the possibility of objective knowledge, all that is left is the propagation of an infinite number of discourses on the provisional character of the individual and society. As Latour (1991) may agree, this has the substance of trickery in that the modification of sociology and social anthropology is ruled out by an appeal that the essential quality of these disciplines lies in a necessary stressing of the duality of the subject and object in human agency (the subject is both knowing and known), as Smart (1982) has noted. In consequence, rather than providing a fertile ground for deriving grounded knowledge about the subject, such a position restricts what can be known. One of the central problems within poststructuralism is that having subsumed agency within discursive practices nothing can be known about how individuals come to occupy specific places within the discursive world. Whereas within postmodernity in general, humankind can only ever acquire contingent knowledge.

This then, is the dilemma within current social science; one chooses either a world view of regularity and the primacy of predictive knowledge within the modernist framework, or considers human experience as being irregular, unpredictable, diverse, contingent and finally subjective. From these starting points there seems little chance for further developments within the social sciences that can reduce our absence of knowledge of the deep underlying structure of human existence; those parts that being universal are beneath culture and discourse. To move forward what is needed is a new perspective within which those aspects of human life characterised by contingency, irregularity and unpredictability can be unfolded within an analysis that accounts for a prediscursive agency. That human mental life is viewed not only from a cultural stance, but also in terms of its evolutionary and adaptive antecedents and enduring features.

In this regard complexity theory can provide a starting point for such a project. Complexity theory shares with postmodern social science the belief in discontinuities, nonlinearity, diversification and unpredictability. Indeed complexity theory can be considered a be a a development within the postmodern natural sciences, particularly in terms of its epistemology. Complexity theory seeks to address critically the concern of modern science with order and predictability and the postmodern concern with diversity and irregularity. Thus offering a critique of both perspectives. With postmodern social science there is agreement regarding the existence of social and cultural lateral and vertical discontinuities (respectively, disjunctions or epistemological dissimilarities within and between given historical epochs), but there is a rejection of the contention that there can be no systematic knowledge gained about human agency. There is retained in common with modern social theory, the possibility of uncovering objective structures or mechanisms that underpin patterns of change with society and culture. In this respect this perspective can be seen to be a way forward from some of the nihilistic aspects of postmodern science without claiming grounds for a belief in linear causal relationships or a systematic predictability with respect to social and cultural life. Complexity theory provides an analysis of disorder and unpredictability whilst simultaneously recovering within social science the possibility of attaining objective knowledge. Where postmodern writing has interpreted disorder and discontinuity as being evidence for the lack of deep structure, complexity theory shows how both order and disorder can arises from determining mechanisms within natural and cultural systems. Uncertainty and unpredictability do not arise because of an absence of objective mechanisms, but are the outcome of their operation.

Complexity theory thus provides a perspective within which certain of the limitations of postmodern writing can be overcome. For example, Foucault's contention that history does not unfold in a continuous manner, but rather by way of a series of epistemological breaks provides one instance of the limitations of an approach that allows no reference to universal characteristics of human agency. For Foucault all knowledge is constrained by the particular epistemic conditions of a given historical epoch. From epoch to epoch these change such that new discursive practices come into being and provide a framework for the possibility of certain kinds of knowing. These give rise to an infrastructure that defines the type of interrelationships that can exist between the subject and the object of their discursive agency, what can be said, by whom and within what kind of institutional context. Foucault argues that over time, these "ways of knowing" change in a discontinuous way such that new forms of knowledge can be accessed. Thus what can be know at any given time is framed within a particular epoch. In his work on the archaeology of knowledge (Foucault 1972) Foucualt contends that Western thought can be considered to have developed by way of three epistemic intervals, each distinct from the any former or subsequent interval. These were held to be the Renaissance, the classical and the modern. The actual differences in patterns of thought depicted by Foucault as being located in these differing epochs is not of importance to this current discussion. The interest here lies in the argument that patterns of thought did not evolve in a continuous manner from one epoch to the next, but rather that the manner of change was such that such that the the ideas of one time were overthrown rapidly by the ideas of the next.

This is an interesting concept, and one which complexity theorists within the social sciences would have no difficulty. For Foucault, however, his focus on the historical context of knowledge limited the extent to which he could have uncovered a cause of nonlinear historical change. In being limited in his analysis to an examination of the empirical conditions of such changes, a documenting of small shifts in discursive practices, he was unable to turn his attention to the possibility of there being nondiscursive mechanisms lying beneath the framework of ideas comprising the discursive world. For Foucualt the possibility of nonlinear change being a characteristic of all complex networks such as human societies could not be considered. Although his findings concerning nonlinear change within human history was an important empirical development within the social sciences, they were constrained theoretically. The reasons why human history changes in a nonlinear way at certain junctures was not dealt with, except descriptively.

Foucault's focus on the relationship between the subject and knowing also gave rise to problems relating to human agency. As Smart (1982) noted, in commenting broadly on the problem of the subject in sociology, Foucault's work provides only a qualified theory of human agency. In limiting his discussion of the subject to the occupation of particular locations in discursive space, Foucault did not account for those aspects of agency that actually led to one subject rather than any other occupying a given space. That is, in Foucault's work primacy was given to the discourse rather than the means by which certain subjects come to occupy a given space at one moment in time. In other words, the way in which certain individuals come to occupy subject positions in discursive formations was ignored. For Foucault, the subject was not important, only the discursive formations at a given historical moment. But once attention turns to the mechanisms through which the subject obtains a particular location, then the prediscursive life of the subject is invoked.

To invoke a prediscursive capacity to human agency is to return to earlier aspects of this analysis. Prediscursive in this context refers to those aspects of human agency and mental life that are non-linguistic, grounded in other moments of our evolutionary past. As has been argued elsewhere in this book, human agency is both determined and incidental. Determined within species level constraints and incidental in terms of its emergent character. Cognitively we are simultaneously embodied and cultural; given and contingent.

The Universal, the Contingent and Nonmodernity

The argument presented so far in within this current analysis of human nature, society and culture has suggested that change within both natural and cultural networks can be understood as arising from causative mechanisms that underpin the multidimensional cognitive, social and cultural world. For example, the way in which species level restrictions on the occurrence of inbreeding and outbreeding may give rise to incest taboos at the cultural level that will vary from one culture to another, depending on prevailing material conditions, was discussed. This means that because an aspect of human nature or culture is determine by underlying causal processes, it does not mean that outcomes can be known with certainty. Cognitive, social that cultural life in part contain elements of unpredictability. The resolution of underlying causal structures and material conditions gives rise to emergent phenomena the exact character of which cannot not be known prior to their appearance as specific outcomes. The species level conditions that in part structure human life, the cultural world of discourse and materiality are interwoven by way of great interconnectiveness between constituent elements. These pathways of interconnectiveness form vectors of feedback and feed-forward between the nested levels of nature, cognition, the social and culture that comprise the greater network of human life. These nested levels are almost decomposable in that change can take place at distinct levels without affecting what happens elsewhere within the nested network, but feedback and feed-forward can trigger change after certain thresholds of change in a specific level are reached (Lee 1997). One consequence of great interconnectivity and the presence of feedback and feed-forward is that although changes taking place at one level can have arisen solely from factors within that level, a complete description of causation cannot take place without including all sources influence from connected levels. Such systems of feedback and feed-forward will give rise to nonlinear change within and between levels, and thus unpredictability and irregularity.

What this indicates is that changes within one level of such a hierarchically structured network can given rise to changes throughout the network. As Lee (1997) has noted, macroscopic structures can be seen to have arisen from microscopic or local interactions. This is to see change at macro-structural levels to have arisen from sets of local interactions; that is, such change is an emergent property of nonlinear processes.

This perspective can thus be seen to have similarities with postmodern concerns with contingency and irregularity. Even Foucault's idea concerning *savoir* and *connaissance* can be seen to mirror the focus in complexity theory on the relationship, respectively, between deep-lying structures and emergent surface level forms of agency. At one level complexity theory provides a basis for uncovering aspects of human agency that reside outside paradigms that view human agency solely from a subjective or cultural perspective. In seeing humankind as being both embodied and contingent there arises the possibility of reforming the relationship between nature and culture that informs postmodern social science without resorting to the problematic, linear notions of objectivity contained within modern social theory. Ideas about interconnectivity contained within complexity theory suggest that all aspects of reality are interwoven; society, culture, mind, materiality and nature. Both modern and postmodern social science have been unable to provide a satisfactory account of the relationship between nature and culture. Postmodern perspectives bracket out nature and consider only the relationship between the subject and culture, whereas modern social science contains the post-Enlightenment interest in the bending of nature to human ends. Complexity theory and human evolutionary theory if combined allow for another approach within which nature and culture are inseparably interconnected. From Latour this can be termed nonmodern social theory. And some founding ideas for this synthesis will be unfolded in the next chapter.

7 Nonmodernity and the Emergence of Cognition and Culture

The history of human kind began at that unknowable time in the past when some unique coming together of certain traits set our ancestors on a path that eventually led to the emergence of our clever, talking, inquisitive, problem-solving and cultural species. The evolutionary path any species finds itself on is both complicated and unlikely. For humankind any small change in direction and we could have ended up as something quite different in form, purpose and capability. The concept of sensitive dependence upon initial conditions formed within complexity theory tells us that this must be the case. If only one small condition of our emergence had been different then it may have been the case that today there would be no human beings sitting down at computers writing books. The path of our evolutionary history has not been smooth, but has instead been an intricate journey of morphological and mental changes in response to shifts in both social and natural environmental conditions. Rather than being a linear progression, the path followed has been turbulent and unpredictable, or, in terms of complexity theory, it has followed the path of a strange attractor. Theses aspects of complex systems, sensitive dependence upon initial conditions and strange attractors, were outlined in chapter two. And these concepts were drawn upon to illustrate the way complexity theory can be used to establish a perspective on human evolution that can account for the readily apparent mosaicism in the fossil record, and the lack so far of a universally accepted theory of the relationship between established patterns of morphological change and engendering environmental conditions.

Environment, Morphology and Cognition

By approaching issues relating to human nature through complexity theory the focus becomes shifted from the pursuit of simple causal relations to one whereby a diversity of conditions becomes the paramount source of human evolutionary changes. In chapter two it was suggested that modern humans arose by the way of an evolutionary history grounded in great diversity in environmental conditions, and that one way of understanding how these conditions could have been encountered was through considering what outcomes may have derived from a nomadic existence. From this perspective, early human encounters with diverse and changing environmental conditions stemmed from migratory behaviour. This in turn led morphological and behavioural divergence between distinct groups, followed by yet further migratory behaviour, continued adaptation and so on. If interbreeding also took place between diverging groups then this too would be a vector of change. And indeed there is some evidence that interbreeding between morphologically different early ancestors did take place.

One further concept from complexity theory can perhaps make the underlying basis of this process somewhat clearer. Stewart (1990) has argued that two key characteristics of complex systems that feature chaotic change are stretching and folding. During the evolution of a complex system points that start off close together can end up very far apart after a finite time interval, but because the system is confined within finite space if stretching continues then some points will have to fold back in on the system and end up once again close to former neighbours. This process will take place on an iterative basis. As a result, from one time interval to the next there will be change in the way each of the points in the system are configured with respect to each other. A dough making machine is a good practical example of this process; the dough is constantly stretched and then folded back in on itself. This is very similar to what has been described with respect to human migration, diversity, re-migration and interbreeding. The system that is humankind has been continually stretched and folded over evolutionary time and geographic space. It is in part this simple process that has given rise to very complex results: a reduction in tooth size, loss of body hair, bipedalism, changes in the upper respiratory tract, changes in skull shape, the enlargement of the brain and many others. Imagine a group of hominids in Africa being represented by a lump of dough. Stretch this dough across Africa and beyond and then fold it back again, then stretch once more and fold back, then stretch and fold, stretch and fold, stretch and fold. What might you get after a few million years?

However, notwithstanding what is being claimed here for the importance of complexity theory to understand some of the process of human evolution, Darwinian natural selection is still a crucial force within processes of change. Complexity theory enables descriptions to be made of fundamental characteristics of dynamic systems, but it does not help in forecasting the types of changes that will arise. The quality of these will arise from the substance of the system not the pattern of its evolutionary path. This point may be easier to grasp if we once again consider weather systems. Although understanding the features of complex systems facilitates the production of more accurate weather forecasts, the actual form weather systems take derives from the physical circumstances of particular geographic areas within a given time period. To make good forecasts we need both complexity theory and a theory of convection. Similarly, an understanding of the establishment of enduring morphological changes within *Homo* cannot be gained without an appreciation of the relationship between species level constraints and specific environmental circumstances. A trait may have emerged as the unintended consequence of a prior adaptive moment (as an exaptation), but for it to have endured it has to have been adaptive within specific environmental circumstances. Each of the morphological characteristics listed above are grounded adaptively. Standing on two legs imparted an advantage, perhaps in terms of reducing heat stress as suggested by Wheeler (1988), as did changes in the upper limb from locomotor or climbing usage to the increased ability to manipulate objects and fashion tools. These and other changes were established adaptively, that is these features endured because they increased individual chances of survival in circumstances of changing environmental conditions (whether encountered through climatic change or from migratory behaviour). They increased the opportunity to survive to reproductive age (i.e. they increased genetic fitness).

At this level of analysis there is no need to draw on complexity theory. However, there are changes to morphology that are so elaborate or intricate that it is extremely difficult to visualise an exact singular circumstances from which they arose. The complicated changes to the respiratory tract that were a key stage in the development of the complex vocalisations of *Homo* are but one example. Some, such as Daniel Dennett and Richard Dawkins, have argued that Darwinian processes are all that is needed, whereas others such as Stephen Gould have proposed processes of exaptation. From the perspective of complexity theory it would seem that Gould and colleagues are perhaps closer to uncovering the essential features of such changes than their rivals.

Complexity theory argues that changes at macro levels occur as a consequences of changes that have taken place deep within systems. In simple terms, changes at the surface occur as an outcome of shifts that take place at the micro level deep within the system. The surface level is some reflection of the internal state of a system. However, different levels of a system do not function separately as there is great interconnectiveness between dissimilar, semiautonomous parts of a complex system (elements that are partly decomposable). Through this interconnectivity feedback and feed-forward takes place on a large scale. Hence, anything happening at one point in the system will have an impact on every other part of the system within finite time. There is no possibility of exclusive development. Parts of the system are semi-decomposable in that they can function partly autonomously, but such decomposability will remain partial. Seen in these terms, it becomes easier to visualise why any specific morphological change cannot be viewed in phenotypic isolation. If one thing changes then something else will experience changes to the number or type of its inputs, and if these change then it has *de facto* experienced a change of environment. In conditions of competition, and assuming hereditary variation, further adaptation will frequently, if not in the vast majority of cases, follow any prior changes in morphology or behaviour. Hence, from complexity theory it can be appreciated that as a consequence of the existence of great interconnectivity between morphological and behavioural characteristics, adaptation involves nonlinear change.

Let us imagine one way parts of this process may have unfolded. Once upon a time in the distant past the first human ancestor stood shakily on two legs and after aeons of time this became the normative trait for the species. This freed the hands and gave an advantage to those individuals whose hands, although less suited to walking or climbing because perhaps they were less robust than usual, turned out to be better than average for picking up objects and manipulating potential foodstuff. Their forbears had also used twigs and such to acquire food, but changes to the hand necessary for improvement in this ability were at that time countered by the need for robustness derived from a walking or climbing function. But once this condition was removed through the adoption of bipedalism, increased dexterity became the primary adaptive trait. Time passed and our mythical ancestor became very good at using tools, but a new constraint arose. Hands became very good at using and shaping objects, but the number of different types of implement and their uses grew in number until the task of remembering which did what and under what circumstances became problematic, and so this constraint in turn became the selective context for further adaptation. Those slightly better at recalling uses and tools were slightly better at using tools for exploiting food sources. In time some consumed more meat than others, and some of those had a smaller gut, and these changes possibly enabled growth in brain size (Aiello and Wheeler 1995). They then became better tool-makers and an ability to symbolise emerged, as discussed in chapter two. So, from one change, bipedalism, there arose a new chain of possible futures for early human ancestors.

Of course this hypothetical scenario is very simplified as in practice each of the changes depicted would have given rise to far more effects than those described here. Bipedalism would have led to changes in hunting or savaging. If Wheeler is right about heat saving then he may also be correct in suggesting that this enabled australopithecines to forage over lager areas. This may have been one important factor in establishing migratory behaviour, the possible importance of which has already been discussed above. Many other interconnected outcomes could be cited, but the key point being made relates to the process rather than any hypothetical proposition concerning substantive links between one trait and another. It is being argued that if one thing is changed then so is another through a network of interconnected effects and outcomes. This process is nonlinear and unpredictable.

This line of reasoning can also be applied to adaptive changes in cognition. As the preceding analysis as shown, the most common contention is that human cognition is modular. It is argued that our mental life forms within a composite structure of modules derived from the differing circumstances of our evolutionary past. Over time an integration of function arose from the development of symbolic reasoning through the objectification of ourselves and the external world under the conditions of social interaction, as discussed in different ways by both Gerald Edelman and Robin Dunbar. Evidence suggests that the first point of departure from primate cognitive norms may have been associated with improved dexterity in hand movements, that in turn led to advances in tool-making and tool use. As this grew more complex it can be supposed, through utilising key ideas from Deacon's (1997) analysis of the emergence of language, that a transition from iconic labelling, the simple naming of objects, led to the emergence of indices denoting associations between objects. Later, symbolisation arose as higher-order references between indices. Deacon (1997) argues that this was the path to language, but this need not be so. There is no obvious reason why such changes in cognition could not have arisen purely in terms of tool-making and tool use, as argued in chapter three. However, being a social species it is likely that this ability formed the basis for sharing increasingly complex ideas, but the relationship between symbolic reasoning and language could not be so directly correlated. As Dunbar has pointed out, the complex social life of all apes sets particular demands regarding patterns of interaction, and an ability to "read minds" imparts a great advantage. A Theory of Mind and a facility to operate with multiple orders of intensionality would be highly adaptive traits. If these were evolving in complexity alongside the emergence of symbolic reasoning then an integration of function would be expected to have arisen by way of feedback and feed-forward. Indeed, an ability to reason abstractly, by way of symbolisation, would clearly enhance both of these traits, whether through conscious or sub-conscious use. And if Wheeler's ideas about bipedalism and the associated increase in the ability to scavenge over greater areas are linked with Dunbar's views on increasing group size and higher demands of grooming, then we can arrive at a clearer idea of the interconnected development of human cognition. From this the key components of development can be suggested: ToM - orders of intensionality - standing up - being cooler - using hands - travelling further - using tools - bigger groups - more grooming - better ToM and orders of intensionality - symbolising - language. However it should be noted that this is not to suggest that these events occurred one after the other as depicted in the list. Improvements in hand movement may have led to expanded territories, as tools would have possibly made it easier to exploit marginal environments. Conversely, seeking to exploit marginal environments may have led to improvements in manual dexterity. If a linear progression is sought then problems of this kind will be encountered. Instead the suggestion here is that ideas from complexity theory suggest that the development or improvement of a trait arose in a nonlinear way from within the complex matrix of influences comprising all the elements listed. From this perspective the order of emergence is less important than the specification of the matrix or network. If the matrix is specified accurately then the order of emergence is a simple empirical question that could, for example, be explored by way of computer simulation. To approach these issues from a non-complex perspective is to open the door to the production of an infinite number of speculative narratives. As each of these would have at least some legitimate status it would be impossible to choose between them. This problem seems to characterise a great deal of research on human origins at this time.

It should be said at this point that the above description of morphological and cognitive evolution is not meant to be exhaustive. Clearly the list of traits and morphological characteristics is confined to only some of those mentioned in the literature. In terms of cognition, the acceptance of a modular model of the mind means that other features of our mental life not mentioned here would also need to be included in any comprehensive account. For example, there would also need to be an account of art and a natural history intelligence. The purpose here was not to be exhaustive, but to draw out more clearly some of the implications of adopting an approach to human evolution based on complexity theory. Especially with regard to the way new adaptive outcomes can emerge from the persistent interconnectiveness that exists between the social or physical environment and morphological and cognitive characteristics.

One theoretical consequence of adopting this approach is the implicit acceptance of the inseparability of nature of cognition. Being a reflection our our evolutionary past, cognition is infused with the products of previous interchanges between environments, morphology and mental life. As Cosmides and Tooby have shown, in some ways we still think with the brain of a stone age hunter-gatherer. And if we look further into our evolutionary past and towards the limbic-brain stem region of our brain, then to some degree we are cognitively other than human. Our mental life is other than modern, and given that our culture is a reflection of our mental life played out in a given environment, then nature is also reflected in culture and thus culture too is in part nonmodern. In terms of social theory this means that it needs to be recognised that nature and culture can never be wholly separated.

Nature and Culture

One important difference that separates humankind from any other member of the animal kingdom is the existence of culture; the knowledge, techniques, practices, customs and institutions that serve to organise and structure our sociality. Unlike other primates, human beings acquire a social status not only instinctively and in behavioural terms, but also through accessing the cognitive and behavioural output of others. As noted in chapter one, Premack and Premack (1994) have pointed out that we not only inherit genes but also environments and knowledge about those environments. This means that ontologically we are both biological and cultural. However, these two components cannot be separated in the sense that it is meaningful to talk about a biological brain and a cultural mind, or that human agency is a product of the cultural world rather than the natural world. Within culture there will always be found the reflection of nature.

This was the central argument presented in chapter five. Incest taboos are not solely cultural phenomenon but are also the reflection of biological rules about inbreeding and outbreeding. Rules about inbreeding exist adaptively as deep-lying mechanisms that in part govern action. They are an adaptive medium through which nature acts upon human agency, an echo of the universal laws of natural selection. Genetically it makes sense for inbreeding to be avoided when outbreeding is possible, so by way of the process of natural selection a mechanism that structures human behaviour appropriately was acquired. But, of course, human beings do not act purely on the basis of instincts, we can also act intentionally by way of rational thought. In consequence there is a theoretical possibility that we could act outside adaptive instinctive traits and engage or not in inbreeding through the exercise of free will. Evidence cited above in chapter five argues that this is less possible than may be supposed, as the medium through which an inbreeding avoidance mechanism appears to operate is through modifying sexual attractiveness between both the members of a household raised together and their parents. This appears to be the the most likely means through which incest avoidance operates on an individual level. In biological terms no other mechanism is necessary, but culturally the situation is somewhat different.

Culture emerged from evolutionary developments in human cognition and social life. In this sense culture is a product of cognition and social behaviour in that it is an outcome of the interweaving of both these products of our evolutionary past. Once cultural practices emerged then these would be a source of feedback to cognition and social behaviour, but initially culture was solely the outcome of the melding of prior outcomes of natural selection acting on morphology and cognition. Culture cannot exist without language so, from a theoretical stance, it is reasonable to mark the arrival of culture as the time when conscious rational reflection on human social interests began to be talked about. The moment of cultural emergence can thus be understood to be the moment when an aspect of mental life became collectively derived and acted out socially. From this moment onwards collective agency began to re-pattern the environment according to shared cognitive and social templates. A self-conscious, collective knowing that operated intentionally to restructure the environment emerged from the inseparable mental and social life derived from prior evolutionary events. But this did not mean that culture acquired infinite boundaries, as the capacity to act was constrained adaptively by what had gone before. From the first moment of its emergence culture was the collective, intentional expression of evolved species level interests.

Over time feedback and feed-forward between culture, cognition, morphology and the intentionally changed environment established a new pattern of co-evolution. Each new evolutionary change occurred as an emergent outcome of this expanded, massively interconnected system. That is, each new outcome occurred by way of an interweaving between constituent, partly decomposable elements comprising cognition, the social and physical environment and cultural practices. Each became represented within the others. For example, culture reflected human mental life in that cognitive modules relating to, say, "looking for cheaters" or the avoidance of incest found cultural expression through the institution of rules, norms and taboos. The individual pre-cultural mind became to be accessed collectively in relation to matters concerning social living, and these formed the basis of cultural practices. Hence rules about cheating and inbreeding became to be inscribed in collective practices. From being facets of individual psychology they became aspects of social and cultural structure.

Given the complex nature of these events it is likely that these emergent outcomes would have varied between one location and another. Differences would arise as the collective expression of a deeplying cognitive trait would unfold within a specific social group located in a given environment. This would mean that, with respect to, say, inbreeding avoidance, associated cultural practices with would emerge in form for each group from the distinctive circumstances of their social and cultural life. Incest taboos would thus vary from one social group to another. Every group would have an incest taboo but everywhere they would be different. Universality and differentiation would sit side by side in the unfolding of cultural practices. An incest taboo, for example, would be simultaneously the expression of nature (the avoidance of inbreeding) and a cultural practice (the collective realisation of this specific cognitive trait in a given set of social and material circumstances). Consequently the form taken by any given outcome would be difficult to predict. In the case of inbreeding this means that although it can be known that some form of incest taboo will always arise within any modern human social group we will never be able to predict theoretically its actual form. In being the outcome of the resolution of diverse elements of human life, cultural practices will be found to be diverse, irregular and unpredictable. Human life unfolds within a nature-culture matrix comprising aspects of the environment, cognition and sociality and in consequence it is a turbulent affair, not given to a definitive, substantive causal analysis in either a contemporary or historical sense.

Nonmodern Life

One of the most important consequences for social theory of the above analysis is the implicit inseparability of nature and culture. Human agency is seen to be simultaneously historical and contingent. The problems with human agency found in the works of many poststructuralist theorists can be seen to have stemmed from a failure to ground the subject in its evolutionary past. As discussed in chapter six, many writers such as Foucault struggled with incomplete theories of the subject. Concerns about the body were disembodied and expressed in purely discursive or phenomenological terms. This is not to suggest that new insights into human nature cannot be derived from the largely French inspired poststructuralist social theory. As stated above, the postmodern movement in general provided an important critique of modern social science and its infatuation with order, predictability and the pursuit of a predictive science of social life. Through drawing attention to the way social and cultural life is infused with disorder, turbulence, contingency and unpredictability the postmodern movement engendered important new perspectives in research and teaching. Nevertheless the claim that we now lived in a discursive world within which objective knowledge is an impossibility, where the individual and society have transcended nature and where everything is now cultural, is misguided. The contingency and unpredictability accurately described by postmodern writers is not the signal of the end of nature, but instead a consequence of its operation.

Complexity theory reveals that outcomes observed at the macro level arise as a consequence of interactions taking place at deep levels within a system. Rain occurs as a result of convection, itself the outcome of a particular configuration of temperature and moisture. It is a simple mechanism that gives rise to a wide variety of complicated effects. Similarly the wide variety of incest taboos that exist globally stem from the expression of a simple rule about inbreeding in a complex world of great interconnectivity between nature, biology and culture. No complete account of incest regulations and prohibitions can be given without reference to the genetic consequences of inbreeding. There can be no complete theory of an aspect of the social and cultural without an account of their embodied roots.

In seeing human agency as an emergent outcome of the interweaving of the environment, cognition, morphology, social life and culture is to simultaneously make a claim for the indivisibility of nature and culture. Instead of focusing social theoretical interest on the subject as both the architect and product of culture, there can instead be a reorientation of interest towards both the subject and culture as emergent outcomes of complex adaptive processes This is not to deny the semi-decomposability of subjectivity, discourse and cultural practices, and thus their partly autonomous character, but rather to stress the final inseparability of the multiple modes of human agency.

As Bruno Latour has argued, we live in a nonmodern world. Although humankind is presently located at a remarkable stage in its evolutionary history when by virtue of possessing a highly integrated mind of enormous sophistication there can be created ideas of seemingly infinite scope and design, and when at times it seems as if either collectively or as individuals people are capable of limitless intended action, there still remains an anchor in the distant past. We are not transcendent over nature; neither cognitively nor morphologically have we past through a watershed of development. There are no disjunctions in nature in that something appears from nowhere. Or to use Daniel Dennett's phrase, there are no sky hooks. Each stage in the evolution of humankind has followed on as a comprehensible outcome of what has occurred before, but not, of course, by way of easily understandable continuous processes. The evolutionary path followed by any species is discontinuous in that outcomes from one moment to the next cannot be known for certain. Evolution follows the path of a strange attractor. It has an unpredictable path of infinite length, but it is contained within finite space. Unexpected things happen, but not the impossible.

As outlined above, each point along the trajectory of a strange attractor is connected through time to all other points; each is a consequence of those it succeeds. Every point is the resolution at a given time of the all the products of interactions between constituent parts of the system. That is, of each moment of feedback and feed-forward of the semi-decomposable elements that comprise a complex system. At times change within such a system is rapid and chaotic, whereas at other times it is stable and ordered, but at all times nothing happens that is not the outcome of the internal operation of the system. For humankind this means that nothing happens that is not the outcome of the operation of nature, mind and culture. Each resides within the other and from this configuration emerges human agency, this is so now and has been the case throughout our evolutionary past. If human life seems more varied and rapidly changing than during any previous time or in comparison with other species then this can be seen to be an outcome of the increased complexity of the base of human agency when compared with previous periods in our evolutionary past, and in comparison with other animals. Humankind can call upon symbolic reasoning and language to structure social life and produce diverse and elaborate patterns of living. Compared to the agency of other species human agency emerges from a base of interconnectivity between not only only nature and behaviour, but also an ability to symbolise the world, a self-conscious awareness based upon social interaction and a shared mental life expressed in cultural practices. Human agency is more diversely based than is the case with other species at this moment in Earth's history, which is to say that it is the outcome of a more massively interconnected system comprising a greater number of constituent elements. This may modify our relationship to nature, but it does not separate us any more than the emergence of culture supplanted all aspects of our individual consciousness.

Overall, the central theme of this book has been to sketch out a possible synthesis of Darwinian natural selection theory and complexity theory, and to show how this could provide new insights into the evolution of cognition and and the character of human agency. Human life has unfolded over time as the outcome of natural selection and as an emergent property of the operation of a complex system. Some evolutionary developments took place by way of classical Darwinian processes, but others have arisen as exaptations; emergent consequences of interaction between dissimilar morphological characteristics, the environment, cognition and social life. At some point culture emerged and this added yet a further compound element to an already complex system. As complexity increased so too did the possibility of turbulence, unpredictability and discontinuous change. This, it has been argued, has been a feature of our evolution and continues to be a feature of human agency , social life and culture in the contemporary world. Life is complex, and predictable change sits side-by side with the confusion of instability. Order and chaos can change places at any moment.

This approach introduces new ideas about the relationship between evolution and human agency. The theoretical division between nature and culture that has been featured within sociology and anthropology almost from their founding moments as modes of inquiry can perhaps be put aside and new avenues explored (or old ones rediscovered). Complexity theory is based upon the concepts of unpredictability and interconnectiveness, so perhaps this approach may provide the means to explore further Latour's claim that we have never been modern. It is hoped that this book may make some small contribution to current attempts to define a nonmodern social theory and form a new outlook on cognition, culture and human agency.

Bibliography

Abdulrazzaq, Y. M., Bener, A., al-Gazali, L. I., al-Khayat, A. I., Micallef, R. and Gaber, T. (1997), 'A study of possible deleterious effects of consanguinity', *Clinical Genetics*, vol. 51(3), pp. 167-173.

Aberle, D. F., Bronfenbrenner, U., Hess, E. H., Miller, D. R., Schneider, D. M. and Spuhler, J. N. (1968), 'The incest taboo and the mating patterns of animals', in P. Bohannan and J. Middleton (eds.), *Marriage, Family and Residence*, The Natural History Press, New York, pp. 3-20.

Aiello, L. and Dunbar, R. I. M. (1993), 'Neocortex size, group size and the evolution of language', *Current Anthropology*, vol. 34, pp. 184-193.

al-Abdulkareem, A. A. and Ballal, S. G. (1998), 'Consanguineous marriage in an urban area of Saudi Arabia: rates and adverse health effects on the offspring', *Journal of Community Health*, vol. 23(1), pp. 75-83.

Alexander, R. D. (1977), 'Natural selection and the analysis of human sociality', *The Changing Scene of the Natural Sciences. Special Publication of the Academy of Natural Sciences*, pp. 283-337.

AlGazali, L. I., Bener, A., Abdulrazzaq, Y. M., Micallef, R., AlKhayat, A. I. and Gaber, T. (1997), 'Consanguineous marriages in the United Arab Emirates', *Journal of Biosocial Science*, vol. 29(4), pp. 491-497.

Alsalem, M. and Rawashdeh, N. (1993), 'Consanguinity in Northern Jordan', *Journal of Biosocial Science*, vol. 25(4), pp. 553-556.

Bauman, Z. (1991), *Modernity and Ambivalence*, Polity Press, Cambridge.

Bittles, A. H., Mason, W. M., Greene, J. and Rao, N. A. (1991), 'Reproductive behavior and health in consanguineous marriages', *Science*, vol. 252, pp. 789-794.

Brace, C. L. (1997), 'Modern human origins: narrow focus or broad spectrum', in G. A. Clark and C. M. Willermet (eds.), *Conceptual Issues in Modern Human Origins Research*, Aldine De Gruyter, New York, pp. 11-27.

Byrne, R. (1995), *The Thinking Ape*, Oxford University Press, Oxford.

Byrne, R. W. and Whiten, A. (eds) (1988), *Machiavellian Intelligence: Social expertise and the evolution of intellect in monkeys, apes and humans*, Clarendon Press, Oxford.

Byrne, R. W. and Whiten, A. (1991), 'Computation and mindreading in primate tactical deception', in A Whiten (ed), *Natural Theories of Mind*, Blackwell, Oxford.

Byrne, R. W. and Whiten, A. (1992), 'Cognitive evolution in primates: Evidence from tactical deception', *Man*, vol. 27, pp. 609-627.

Cann, R., Stoneking, M. and Wilson, A. (1987), 'Mitochondrial DNA and human evolution', *Nature*, vol. 325, pp. 31-36.

Clarke, R. J. (1990), 'The Ndutu cranium and the origin of *Homo sapiens*', *Journal of Human Evolution*, vol. 19, pp. 699-736.

Cohen, A. P. (1994), *Self Consciousness. An alternative anthropology of identity.*, Routledge, London.

Corvinas, G. (1976), 'Prehistoric exploration at Hadar, Ethiopia', *Nature*, vol. 261, pp. 571-572.

Cosmides, L. (1989), 'The logic of social exchange: has natural selection shaped how humans reason? Studies with the Wason selection task', *Cognition*, vol. 31, pp. 187-276.

Cosmides, L. and Tooby, J. (1989), 'Evolutionary psychology and the generation of culture, part II, case study: A computational theory of social exchange', *Ethology and Sociobiology*, vol. 10, pp. 51-97.

Cosmides, L. and Tooby, J. (1992), 'Cognitive adaptations for social exchange', in J. H. Barkow, L. Cosmides and J. Tooby (eds.), *The Adapted Mind*, Oxford University Press, New York, pp. 163-228.

Dawkins, R. (1976), *The Selfish Gene*, Oxford University Press, Oxford.

Dawkins, R. (1982), *The Extended Phenotype: The gene as the unit of selection*, Freeman, Oxford.

Deacon, T. (1997), *The Symbolic Species: The co-evolution of language and the human brain*, Allen Lane, London.

Dean, A. (1997), *Chaos and Intoxication: Complexity and adaptation in the structure of human nature*, Routledge, London.

Dennett, D. (1988), 'The intentional stance in theory and practice', in R. W. Byrne and A. Whiten (eds), *Machiavellian Intelligence: Social expertise and the evolution of intellect in monkeys, apes and humans*, Clarendon Press, Oxford, pp. 180-202.

Dennett, D. (1995), *Darwin's Dangerous Idea: Evolution and the meanings of life*, Penguin, London.

Dunbar, R. (1996), *Grooming, Gossip and the Evolution of Language*, Faber and Faber Ltd., London.

Durham, W. H. (1991), *Co-evolution: Genes, culture and human diversity*, Stanford University Press, Stanford.

Edelman, G. (1992), *Bright Air, Brilliant Fire: On the matter of the mind*, Penguin, London.

Edelman, G. M. (1989), *The Remembered Present: A biological theory of consciousness*, Basic Books, New York.

Edmond, M. and De Braekeleer, M. (1993), 'Inbreeding effects on fertility and sterility: a case-control study in Saguenay-Lac-Saint-Jean (Quebec, Canada) based on a population registry 1838-1971', *Annals of Human Biology*, vol. 20(6), pp. 545-555.

Eyre Walker, A., Smith, N. H. and Smith, J. M. (1999), 'How clonal are human mitochodria?', *Proceedings of the Royal Society of London, Series B*, vol. 266(1418), pp. 477-483.

Falk, D. (1983), 'Cerebral cortices of East African early hominids', *Science*, vol. 222, pp. 1072-1074.

Fortes, M. (1949), *The Web of Kinship among the Tallensi*, Oxford University Press, Oxford.

Foucault, M. (1972), *The Archaeology of Knowledge*, Pantheon, New York.

Freud, S. (1960), *Totem and Taboo*, Routledge and Kegan Paul, London.

Frost, G. T. (1980), 'Tool behaviour and the origins of laterality', *Journal of Human Evolution*, vol. 9, pp. 447-459.

Gardner, H. (1983), *Frames of Mind: The theory of multiple intelligences*, Basic Books, New York.

Giddens, A. (1990), *The Consequences of Modernity*, Polity Press, Cambridge.

Goody, J. (1956), 'A comparative approach to incest and adultery', *British Journal of Sociology*, vol. 7, pp. 286-305.

Goody, J. (1968), 'A comparative approach to incest and adultery', in P. Bohannan and J. Middleton (eds.), *Marriage, Family and Residence*, The Natural History Press, New York.

Gould, S. J. and Eldredge, N. (1993), 'Punctuated equilibrium comes of age', *Nature*, vol. 366, pp. 223-227.

Gould, S. J. and Lewontin, R. (1979), 'The spandrels of San Marco and the panglossian paradigm: A critique of the adaptationist programme', *Proceedings of the Royal Society*, vol. B205, pp. 581-598.

Gould, S. J. and Vrba, E. (1982), 'Exaptation: A missing term in the science of form', *Paleobiology*, vol. 8, pp. 4-15.

Hagelberg, E., Goldman, N., Lio, P., Whelan, S., Schiefenhovel, W., Clegg, J. B. and Bowden, D. K. (1999), 'Evidence for mitochondrial DNA recombination in a human population of island Melanesia', *Proceedings of the Royal Society of London, Series B*, vol. 266(1418), pp. 485-492.

Hoodfar, E. and Teebi, A. S. (1996), 'Genetic referrals of Middle Eastern origin in a western city: inbreeding and disease profile', *Journal of Medical Genetics*, vol. 33(3), pp. 212-215.

Hublin, J. (1985), 'Human fossils from the North African middle pleistocene and the origin of *Homo sapiens*', in E. Delson (ed), *Ancestors: The hard evidence*, Alan Liss, New York, pp. 283-288.

Hublin, J. (1992), 'Recent human evolution in Northwestern Africa', *Philosophical Transactions, Royal Society of London, Series B*, vol. 337, pp. 193-200.

Humphrey, N. (1976), 'The social function of intellect', in P. P. G. Bateson and R. A. Hinde (eds), *Growing Points in Ethology*, Cambridge University Press, Cambridge, pp. 303-317.

Jaber, L., Bailey Wilson, J. E., Hajyehia, M., Hernandez, J. and Shohat, M. (1994), 'Consanguineous matings in an Israeli-Arab Community', *Archives of Pediatrics and Adolescent Medicine*, vol. 148(4), pp. 412-415.

Jain, V. K., Nalini, P., Chandra, R. and Srinivasan, S. (1993), 'Congenital malformations, reproductive wastage and consanguineous mating', *Australian and New Zealand Journal of Obstetrics and Gynaecology*, vol. 33(1), pp. 33-36.

Jancar, J. and Johnston, S. J. (1990), 'Incest and Mental Handicap', *Journal of Mental Deficiency Research*, vol. 34, pp. 483-490.

Kauffman, S. A. (1993), *The Origins of Order. Self Organization and Selection in Evolution.*, Oxford University Press, Oxford.

Khlat, M. (1989), 'Inbreeding effects on fetal growth in Beirut, Lebanon', *American Journal of Physical Anthropology*, vol. 80(4), pp. 481-484.

Khoury, M. J., Cohen, B. H., Chase, G. A. and Diamond, E. L. (1987a), 'An epidemiologic approach to the evaluation of the effect of inbreeding on prereproductive mortality', *American Journal of Epidemiology*, vol. 25(2), pp. 251-262.

Khoury, M. J., Cohen, B. H., Diamond, E. L., Chase, G. A. and McKusick, V. A. (1987c), 'Inbreeding and prereproductive mortality in the Old Order Amish. III. Direct and indirect effects of inbreeding', *American Journal of Epidemiology*, vol. 125(3), pp. 473-483.

Khoury, M. J., Cohen, B. H., Newill, C. A., Bias, W. and McKusick, V. A. (1987b), 'Inbreeding and prereproductive mortality in the Old Order Amish. II. Genealogic epidemiology of prereproductive mortality', *American Journal of Epidemiology*, vol. 125(3), pp. 462-472.

Kiel, L. D. and Elliott, E. (1996), *Chaos Theory in the Social Sciences: Foundations and applications*, The University of Michigan Press, Ann Arbor.

Kimura, D. (1976), 'The neurological basis of language qua gestures', in H. Whitaker and H. A. Whitaker (eds.), *Current Trends in Neurolinguistics*, Academic Press, New York.

Klein, R. G. (1989), *The Human Career: Human biological and cultural origins*, The University of Chicago Press, Chicago.

Knight, C. (1991), *Blood Relations: Menstruation and the origins of culture*, Yale University Press, New Haven.

Krishan, G. (1986), 'Effect of parental consanguinity on anthropometric measurements among the Sheikh Sunni Muslim boys of Delhi', *American Journal of Physical Anthropology*, vol. 70(1), pp. 69-73.

Kunstadter, P. (1964), 'Demographic variability and preferential marriage patterns', *American Journal of Physical Anthropology*, vol. 21, pp. 511-519.

Kuper, A. (1994), *The Chosen Primate*, Harvard, Cambridge, MA.

Latour, B. (1993), *We Have Never Been Modern*, Harvester Wheatsheaf, Hemel Hempstead.

Leakey, R. E. and Walker, A. (1989), 'Early *Homo erectus* from West Lake Turkana, Kenya', in G. Giacobini (ed), *Hominidae, Proceedings of the 2nd International Congress of Human Paleontology*, Jaca Book, Milan, pp. 209-215.

Lecours, A. R. and Joanette, Y. (1980), 'Linguistic and other aspects of paroxysmal aphasia', *Brain and Language*, vol. 10, pp. 1-23.

Lee, M. E. (1997), 'From enlightenment to chaos: Toward nonmodern social theory', in R. A. Eve, S. Horsfall and M. E. Lee (eds.), *Chaos, Complexity and Sociology: Myths, models and theories*, Sage, Thousand Oaks, pp. 15-29.

Levi-Strauss, C. (1969), *The Elementary Structures of Kinship*, Eyre and Spottiswoode, London.

Lieberman, P. (1988), 'Language, intelligence and rule-governed behaviour', in H. J. Jerison and I. Jerison (eds.), *Intelligence and Evolutionary Biology*, Springer, Berlin.

Lieberman, P. (1994), 'The origins and evolution and language', in T. Ingold (ed), *Companion Encyclopedia of Anthropology*, Routledge, London, pp. 108-132.

Lieberman, P. and Crelin, E. S. (1971), 'On the speech of Neanderthal Man', *Linguistic Inquiry*, vol. 11, pp. 203-222.

Livingstone, F. B. (1958), 'Anthropological implications of sickle cell gene distribution in West Africa', *American Anthropologist*, vol. 60, pp. 533-562.

Lorenz, E. N. (1963), 'Deterministic nonperiodic flows', *Journal of Atmospheric Science*, vol. 29, pp. 130-141.

Malinowski, B. (1929), *The Sexual Life of Savages in North-Western Melanesia*, Routledge and Kegan Paul, London.

Malinowski, B. (1959), 'Culture', in E. R. A. Seligman (ed), *Encyclopaedia of the Social Sciences*, Macmillan, London, pp. 629-630.

Malinowski, B. (1960), *Sex and Repression in Savage Society*, Routledge and Kegan Paul, London.

Manktelow, K. I. a. O., D. E. (1987), 'Reasoning and rationality', *Mind and Language*, vol. 2, pp. 199-219.

Mills, C. W. (1959), *The Sociological Imagination*, Oxford University Press, New York.

Mithen, S. (1998), *The Prehistory of the Mind: A search for the origins of art, religion and science*, Phoenix, London.

Morgan, E. (1990), *The Scars of Evolution: What our bodies tell us about human origins*, Souvenir Press Ltd., London.

Morgan, E. (1997), *The Aquatic Ape Hypothesis: The most credible theory of human evolution*, Souvenir Press Ltd., London.

Morgan, R. (1982), *The Aquatic Ape*, Souvenir Press Ltd., London.

Murdock, G. P. (1949), *Social Structure*, Macmillan, New York.

Nabulsi, A. (1995), 'Mating patterns of the Abbad tribe in Jordan', *Social Biology*, vol. 42(3-4), pp. 162-174.

Odling-Smee, F. J. (1994), 'Niche construction, evolution and culture', in T. Ingold (ed), *Companion Encyclopedia of Anthropology*, Routledge, London, pp. 162-196.

Plotkin, H. (1994), *The Nature of Knowledge*, Penguin, London.

Premack, D. and Premack, A. J. (1994), 'Why animals have neither culture nor history', in T. Ingold (ed), *Companion Encyclopedia of Anthropology*, Routledge, London, pp. 350-365.

Rattray, R. F. (1929), *Ashanti Law and Constitution*, Oxford University Press, Oxford.

Reddy, B. M. (1992), 'Inbreeding effects on reproductive outcome: a study based on a large sample from the endogamous Vadde of Kolleru Lake andhra Pradesh, India', *Human Biology*, vol. 64(5), pp. 659-682.

Rightmire, G. P. (1990), *The Evolution of Homo erectus*, Cambridge University Press, Cambridge.

Ruelle, D. (1993), *Chance and Chaos*, Penguin, London.

Saha, H., Hamad, R. E. and Mohamed, S. (1990), 'Inbreeding effects on reproductive outcome in a Sudanese population', *Human Heredity*, vol. 40(4), pp. 208-212.

Schepers, G. W. H. (1946), 'The endocranial casts of the South African ape-men', in R. Broom and G. W. H. Schepers (eds), *The South African Fossil Ape-Men: The Australopithecinae, Transvaal museum memoirs*, pp. 153-272.

Schepers, G. W. H. (1950), 'The brain casts of the recently discovered *Plesianthropus* skulls', in R. Broom, J. T. Robinson and G. W. H. Schepers (eds), *Sterkfontein Ape-man, Plesianthropus, Transvaal museum memoirs*, pp. 85-117.

Schneider, D. M. (1976), 'The meaning of incest', *The Journal of the Polynesian Society*, vol. 85, pp. 149-169.

Shami, S. A., Qadeer, T., Schmitt, L. H. and Bittles, A. H. (1991), 'Consanguinity, gestational period and anthropometric measurements at birth in Pakistan', *Annals of Human Biology*, vol. 18(6), pp. 523-527.

Shepher, J. (1971), 'Mate selection among second-generation Kibbutz adolescents and adults: Incest avoidance and negative imprinting', *Archives of Sexual Behavior*, vol. 1, pp. 293-307.

Shepher, J. (1983), *Incest: A biosocial view*, Academic Press, New York.

Sivakumaran, T. A. and Karthikeyan, S. (1997), 'Effects of inbreeding on reproductive losses in Kota tribe', *Acta Geneticae, Medicae, et Gemellologiae*, vol. 46(2), pp. 123-128.

Smart, B. (1982), 'Foucault, sociology and the problem of human agency', *Theory and Society*, vol. 11(2), pp. 121-290.

Sokal, A. and Bricmont, J. (1998), *Intellectual Postures: Postmodern philosopher's abuse of science*, Profile Books Ltd., London.

Stringer, C. and Gamble, C. (1993), *In Search of the Neanderthals: Solving the puzzle of human origins*, Thames and Hudson Inc., New York.

Stuss, D. and Benson, D. F. (1986), *The Frontal Lobes*, Raven Press, New York.

Susman, R. L. (1987), 'Pygmy chimpanzees and common chimpanzees: Models for the behavioral ecology of the earliest hominids', in W. G. Kingsley (ed), *Evolution of Human Behaviour*, State University of New York Press, Albany, pp. 73.

Tobias, P. V. (1981), *The Evolution of the Human Brain, Intellect and Spirit*, in: *1st Andrew Abbie Memorial Lecture*, University of Adelaide Press, Adelaide.

Tobias, P. V. (1983), 'Recent advances in the evolution of the hominids with especial reference to brain and speech', *Pontificiae Academiae Scientarum Scripta Varia*, vol. 50, pp. 85-140.

Tobias, P. V. (1994), 'The evolution of early hominids', in T. Ingold (ed), *Companion Encyclopedia of Anthropology*, Routledge, London, pp. 33-78.

Trinkaus, E. (1986), 'The Neanderthals and the origins of modern humans', *Annual Review of Anthropology*, vol. 15, pp. 193-218.

Van den Berghe, P. (1979), *Human Family Systems*, Elsevier, New York.

Wahab, A. and Ahmad, M. (1996), 'Biosocial perspectives of consanguineous marriages in rural and urban Swat, Pakistan', *Journal of Biosocial Science*, vol. 28(3), pp. 305-313.

Wason, P. C. (1972), 'Reasoning', in B. M. Foss (ed), *New Horizons in Psychology 1*, Penguin, Harmondsworth.

Westermarck, E. A. (1894), *The History of Human Marriage*, The Macmillan Company, London.

Wheeler, P. (1991a), 'The thermoregulatory advantages of hominid bipedalism in open equatorial environments', *Journal of Human Evolution*, vol. 21, pp. 107-115.

Wheeler, P. (1991b), 'The influence of bipedalism on the energy and water budgets of early hominids', *Journal of Human Evolution*, vol. 21, pp. 117-136.

Wolf, A. P. (1966), 'Childhood association, sexual attraction and the incest taboo: A Chinese case', *American Anthropologist*, vol. 68, pp. 883-898.

Wolf, A. P. (1970), 'Childhood association and sexual attraction: A further test of the Westermarck hypothesis', *American Anthropologist*, vol. 72, pp. 503-515.

Wynn, T. (1994), 'Tools and tool behaviour', in T. Ingold (ed), *Companion Encyclopedia of Anthropology*, Routledge, London, pp. 133-161.

Yaqoob, M., Gustavson, K. H., Jalil, F., Karlberg, J. and Iselius, L. (1993), 'Early childhood health in Lahore, Pakistan, 2, inbreeding', *Acta Paediatrica*, vol. 82, pp. 17-26.